D1322798

Improving Productivity & Performance in the Hospitality Sector: Getting It Done!

John Heap, Tracy Todd & Mike Dillon

ISBN:

978-0-9572726-5-1

i

DEDICATION

This book is dedicated to all those who, over the years, have provided us with the services – and service - we need to be able to work effectively whilst away from home.

Mike Dillon, John Heap, Tracy Todd

CONTENTS

John Heap, Tracy Todd & Mike Dillon

ACKNOWLEDGMENTS

We want to acknowledge the help of the members of the World Confederation of Productivity Science whose conversations, discussions and debates have helped us think through the issues that have shaped this book.

THE GETTING IT DONE SERIES

This is part of a series of books from the Institute of Productivity aimed at providing a comprehensive, practical approach to the measurement and improvement of performance and productivity, at organisational and at national level.

These books are aimed at a range of audiences – from policy-makers and strategists, through project officers and facilitators to (especially) the practitioners - those responsible for 'Getting It Done'.

The books introduce and explain relevant concepts and theory but they always take the reader through specific approaches, techniques and examples that act as a template for practical implementation.

The books are designed to be pragmatic ... to give real world approaches and solutions. We have also designed the book to be brief ... and to be complementary. Though each book stands alone, maximum benefit comes from applying the concepts across the series of books – Getting It (All) Done.

www.instituteofproductivity.com

The Institute of Productivity is a think-tank, publishing house and strategic consultancy focusing on the trade and business benefits of addressing all of Social, Environmental & Economic (SEE) Productivities.

The Institute of Productivity provides high quality education, training and support resources to help governments, organisations and individuals create the potential for high productivity ... and then exploit that potential and deliver sustained, high performance.

SECTION 1

1 INTRODUCTION

What is it that organisations set out to do?

Well, of course, it depends on the type of organisation we are looking at. They may be attempting to make some money (maybe even lots of money), to make a mark on the world in a given area, to bring together people with a common interest, or to provide a service they believe society needs.

The hospitality industry's primary aim is making money, but many also want to make a positive contribution to the world through their social, environmental and economic policies.

Whatever the purpose of an organisation, however, one assumes they want to do it to the best of their ability This means they have to perform ... and to do this they need to have plans, aims and goals ... that they have created as their 'route map' to their chosen destination, their foreseeable set of achievements. To ensure they remain on course, they have to have ways of knowing if they are achieving those plans, meeting those aims and reaching those goals.

If they find they are off target, they need to take corrective action. Even if they are on target, they might have to keep making (small) adjustments. This is what planning and control is all about. This is what managers do ... they plan, organise, measure and control. And all organisations have managers – even those that are designed to be non-hierarchical. The people who 'manage' (e.g. Hotel General Managers, Rooms Division, Food & Beverage

Managers) carry out those functions of planning, organising, measuring and controlling … or, more than likely, the organisation is not being successful.

Perhaps a small correction is necessary. The act of managing might be carried out in some collective or distributed fashion. So perhaps 'managers' do not always exist … but certainly the functions and processes of management do.

This is not a management text … in so far as it makes no attempt to cover all of the functions and processes of management. We are looking at the specific function of measurement – and management - of performance. However this is such an important management function that it is worth taking some time to explore and understand it …. and to learn how it can be carried out effectively. If you cannot measure performance effectively, you cannot manage effectively. Figure 1-1 represents this process of using performance measurement as the basis of improvement.

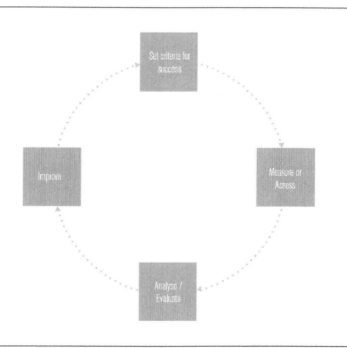

Figure 1-1 The use of performance measurement as the basis of improvement

Performance measurement is not an end in itself: it is a step on the road to performance and productivity improvement, to organisational growth and development – and success. Performance measurement must not be a 'top-down' process to identify blame; it must be an all-encompassing process to identify areas for improvement and opportunities for innovation.

The measured results provide valuable information to those who need to take improvement decisions - whether they be at the operational or strategic level - relating to the processes and activities being measured. With the measurement data, these decision-makers are able to take decisions on the basis of evidence rather than hunch, whim or 'instinct'.

The commonest 'performance measure' in business relates to financial performance ... and many organisations have whole reporting and control regimes based around the measurement of actual and planned performance according to the annual budget (and its monthly or weekly breakdown).

Clearly in the hospitality industry - as in any business - measuring only financial performance would give a very unbalanced view of the performance of the business. Businesses do not set out with the primary aim of managing their budget - this is just one of the many things they have to do to fulfil their primary role of providing excellent service.

Hotels have always used a variety of measures to assess the performance of their business - and externally, institutes like the AA and Mobile have graded the industry based on the provision and delivery of service. For example in the UK orange star ratings indicate accommodation which has been assessed by the AA. In collaboration with VisitEngland, VisitScotland and VisitWales, the AA has developed Common Quality Standards for inspecting and rating hotels and guest accommodation. These standards and rating categories are now applied throughout the British Isles. Any hotel or guest house applying for AA recognition receives an unannounced visit from an AA inspector to check standards.

Standards are categorized by numbers, letters and stars as outlined below:

4★	Hotel
4★G	Guest Accommodation
4★A	Serviced Apartments
4★S	Self-Catering
4★h	Hostel
4★C	Campus
B	Budget

All categories are broken down further, For example hotels are segmented into hotels, small hotels, country house hotels, town house hotels and metro hotels.

Within each category, the AA grades the sector from one to five stars based on established standards and criterion. For example, a five star hotel is expected to have more than twenty rooms, (100% of which should be ensuite), have at least one restaurant, be open 24 hours a day, 365 days per year, and be licensed to serve alcohol. However, a five star hotel also needs to show it has enhanced services and facilities for the guests. It has to show exceptional and proactive customer care and all areas of operation should meet the 'Five Star' level of quality for cleanliness, maintenance, hospitality, and for the quality of physical facilities and delivery of services.

This type of external 'quality standard' reassures potential guests that their expectations for 'quality' ought to be met and forms a basis for complaints if standards are not met.

AA grading ensures a hotel is aware of how it should be performing. However, AA grading is a 'summative assessment' – it measures the end result of all the internal operations and processes that go to make up the running of the establishment. The hotel itself has to ensure that those operations and processes are planned, executed and controlled to deliver that summative assessment. This almost certainly means there is a need for 'formative assessment' - internal, intermediate measures of quality and performance that keeps everything on track to deliver the end services to guests and ensures favourable reviews by inspectors.

Later on in this book, we shall take a look at the Balanced Scorecard which is one of the more common, 'comprehensive' performance measures … designed, as the name suggests, to offer a balanced view of performance against a range of criteria. Before such techniques were widely known and implemented, 'balanced' measures were often less formalised, less structured … and therefore less effective. Thus measurement regimes built on the concept of 'balance' have added a (useful) structure to a practice (of using multiple performance measures) that was already reasonably widespread.

As the General Manager or CEO of a hospitality business, be it a hotel, restaurant or fast food outlet, an executive needs to know certain things. But, independent of the business, a good CEO knows that the important, high level things depend on lots of little things happening at lower levels. This good CEO knows there is a small number of questions he/she can ask of those at the operational level that should provide a good guide as to what 'his' or 'her' macro level will look like next time it is reported. And this good CEO knows that sometimes waiting for these lower level actions (and measures) to 'trickle up' to the macro level is the wrong thing to do. If the macro measures look wrong - if the organisation is under-performing – the harm has been done. Similarly, a good manager will have a number of key issues and key measures that he/she attends to on a regular basis - serving as the 'barometer' of performance.

So, though the 'conventional wisdom' is that the higher level measures we build on the basis of our strategy have to be 'translated' for lower levels of management into lower levels of measurement, some General Managers are smart enough to know that the reverse is sometimes a better approach. Sometimes it is smarter to ask to see the lower level measures and to translate these into their effects on the higher level measures still to emerge.

Notice that sometimes we use the word 'measure' and sometimes we use the term 'indicator'. These are broadly interchangeable but there is an important distinction. Clearly, a 'measure' is just that - a reading of the magnitude of a certain factor we are interested in (output, quality, time, etc). The measure is a direct reading to a known accuracy and is difficult to argue with … someone else using the same equipment to gauge the same factor should arrive at the same measure. However, we might be using this measure to assess (in part) a wider attribute, a larger factor. If our 'measure' does not represent the whole of this wider factor, then it becomes merely an 'indicator' of the magnitude of that wider factor.

Similarly we might have a qualitative assessment of some factor - guest satisfaction, for example - arrived at by a survey; this, again, is an indicator since it does not, indeed cannot, measure all the of the factors inherent in such a broad term as guest satisfaction. Indicators are useful - but they do need to be addressed by someone who knows the wider context. General Managers who are making judgements based on performance data must know what the data means ... and what it does not necessarily mean. The data must be filtered through their knowledge and experience.

Finally, the kind of indicator we need to fully understand what is going on might be a composite indicator of some kind, arrived at by combining or manipulating data in some way. This is how we get:

Measures of Efficiency or Productivity (ratio of output per unit of input)

... and, often, it is helpful to compare actual performance with planned performance to get:

Measures of Effectiveness (how close to the target or goal set)

We do not only measure the critical things... all the measures we take are not critical. There are all sorts of reasons why we might want - temporarily or more permanently - to measure non-critical, but important things. It is, however, important that we do identify all of those measures that ARE critical.

Too often businesses take a 'half-hearted' approach to performance measurement. They use performance measures because the data exist and there are obvious measures arising from the process - such as the number of staff arriving late for work. Sometimes they use particular measures because they have always used them. These may be valid reasons for using a particular set of performance measures - but they may not!
We must not forget that measuring costs money. Any measurement regime will incur some cost ... and some, such as automated, real-time, staff lateness monitoring and absenteeism system might be fairly expensive to install. Of course we have to balance the cost of measurement with its utility ... but as the old adage put it ... "If you think measurement is expensive, look at the costs of not measuring".

If you do not measure performance, you have no idea of where you are in relation to plan, where you are in relation to those factors you have decided are critical to your further progress and development.

Measurement is only effective, of course, when it leads to some kind of action. We said above that measurement is the basis of corrective action and control - the measure and its comparison with the plan or target allows such corrective action to be determined.

But the best measures do more. They actually change behaviour. When people (individuals or groups) know their performance is being reported upon - and where such individuals or groups have control over performance - they are likely to change their performance to make the measures 'better'. For example, if an apprentice chef is being observed preparing a particular dish, and knows on that one day he will be marked for any deviation from the set preparation and/or presentation, he/she will make every effort to ensure accuracy …whereas, if unobserved, he/she might not be as careful. However, true behavioural change has not taken place, rather a test has been passed. Alternatively, if a waiter is told 'the dish of the day' is being monitored as to the number of dishes sold, and his/her bonus at the end of the month will be affected by it, then effort to sell the one dish will be higher for that month, as opposed to improving overall upselling skills.

This means that you had better be sure that your measures will drive behaviour in the right direction. Many measures result in sub-optimal behaviour, often because the measures used are not 'balanced'. This is why measuring profit is generally regarded as necessary but not sufficient for a profit-making organisation. The measurement of profit needs to be balanced by the use of other measures addressing other critical performance issues … perhaps issues which will result in future, enhanced profits.

If we have a complete and appropriate set of indicators, they should be able to help us answer simple but vital questions such as:

- ▶ **Where are we?**
- ▶ **Where do we want to be (and when)?**
- ▶ **How are we going to get there cost effectively?**

Remember, though, that these questions are 'of their time'. The answers will be different at different phases of an organisation's development. This means that performance indicators will change over time … to reflect the changing environment and the changing situation of the organisation.

Of course in the hospitality industry, we have a particular reason for measuring performance. We have already mentioned that there are external measures set up by institutions such as AA or Mobile which can increase the number of customers and overall profit with their grading standards. Whether or not a business agrees that this external regime is truly effective, it exists for a purpose. To ignore it would be folly. What good hospitality leaders do is to recognise it .. and incorporate it into a wider performance measurement and management regime that meets both the external - and the business's own - needs.

The challenge, that this book aims to address, is to know what to measure … now.

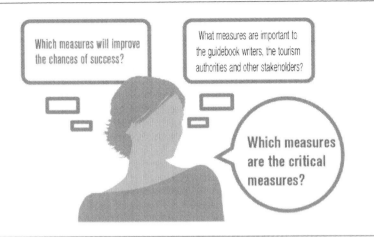

We tackle this challenge by first explaining why many performance management schemes fail (unfortunately, they do); we then go on to explore the concepts of key and critical performance indicators ... and, perhaps most importantly, in the second half of this book, we take you through the entire process of devising and implementing key and critical performance indicators for your business, using a case study of a particular (fictitious) hotel so you can see how all the measures - and measurement processes - link together to give an overall understanding of the hotel and its performance.

Note: Within the hotels sector, the term 'performance management' can often be used to refer to a process of 'appraisal' of individuals. When we use the term, we are considering a much wider programme where the 'performance' of whole processes, whole systems and ultimately a whole organisation is measured or assessed.

John Heap, Tracy Todd & Mike Dillon

2 NATIONAL and INTERNATIONAL CONTEXTS FOR PERFORMANCE MEASUREMENT

Tourism and hospitality are huge businesses internationally. In some countries they are even the main source of direct income and thus major contributors to GDP. Therefore, ensuring and assuring the performance of the hospitality sector is important to many nations. A beach resort in Sharm Alsheik, Egypt, now competes not only internally with Luxor and Alexandria, but also internationally, with resorts in Turkey, Greece and Cyprus. It is important, therefore, at the organisational/corporate level to get the internal and external standards of performance and service right in order to differentiate one's business and become the hotel/restaurant (chain) of preference. At the national level, it is clearly in the interests of governments to ensure the reputation of the overall hospitality sector as offering 'quality' and 'value' when compared to competing tourist destinations.

This is why most countries have some sort of system for focusing attention on how well their hotels and restaurants perform. If they do not, it is likely they will align with a system of a neighbouring country or continent.

Meeting global standards and gaining certification is one of the external methods of achieving recognition. Even though this is true, and can be seen as part of the general trend towards 'openness', detailed data on the performance of organisations is not made available to the public. They have to rely on the kind of summary grading we referred to before undertaken by organisations such as the AA, Mobile, or Michelin and assume that these summary measures/grades are a reasonable indicator of the underlying performance in key areas.

Other external measurements, which in turn affect internal performance measurement, include measures of environmental performance. The World Travel and Tourism Council, (WTTC), has created a 'hotel carbon measurement initiative', to provide consistent assessments of such environmental performance. Twenty-three leading global hotel companies, (over 15,000 hotels world-wide), have signed up to their scheme. The WTTC provides the know-how, system and tool kit. At the top level, each hotel group commits to reduce their carbon emissions. Then throughout each hotel, changes of behaviour and performance are initiated to reach the targets set.

There are many systems to support internal data comparisons, as well as the bespoke internal strategic and operational measurements. There are basically two areas that need to be measured to give an overview of how well an organisation is performing - financial and operational performance. Financial measures for the hospitality or tourism sector are similar to those for any other business - measuring (gross and net) profits, asset performance, accounts receivable etc. Operational measures look in more detail at each 'department', i.e. what is the occupancy rate for hotel rooms, the average selling price of a room, the seat occupancy rate of a restaurant, the level of spend by customers when they visit the bar, etc.

The International Context

Internationally, hotels have very similar internal measures, although targets and how they achieve them, will differ based on what the aim of the business is. Some countries have government standards set up, comparable to the British Food & Safety Hygiene Standards, though many rely on 'sector standards' set and operated by associations and recognised bodies.

Switzerland established the first non-government, formal hotel classification in 1979· Consequently, it influenced Austria and Germany and eventually led to the formation of the HOTREC (Hotels, Restaurants & Cafés in Europe) - an umbrella organization for 39 associations from 24 European countries. In 2007 HOTREC launched the European Hospitality Quality scheme (EHQ) which has since accredited the existing national inspection bodies for hotel rating.

Furthermore, under the patronage of HOTREC, the hotel associations of Austria, Czech Republic, Germany, Hungary, Netherlands, Sweden, and Switzerland created the **Hotelstars Union**, and since then many more east and western countries have joined the association.

The European Hotelstars Union system has a catalogue of criteria which must be met, with 21 qualifications and 270 elements, where some are mandatory for a star and others optional. The main criteria relate to quality management, wellness and sleeping accommodation. To establish a rating of between three to five stars, the Hotelstars Union will use an un-announced 'mystery guest' to check the service quality regularly.

With the increase of television chefs and the popularisation of food programmes, the international Michelin grading system is often quoted, particularly for restaurants, although it is also used to inspect hotels. It is a industry-recognised standard offering a high level of publicity to any accredited restaurant and has been established for 100 years. Fundamental to the process are the repeat visits by anonymous Michelin Inspectors to test meals and stay overnight in hotels without the owners/managers knowing. Because the award of Michelin stars is rare, it is seen as an important accolade - one of the highest honours in the industry.

> 'One star indicates a very good restaurant in its category, offering cuisine prepared to a consistently high standard. A good place to stop on your journey. Two stars denotes excellent cuisine, skilfully and carefully crafted dishes of outstanding quality. Worth a detour. Three stars reward exceptional cuisine where diners eat extremely well, often superbly. Distinctive dishes are precisely executed, using superlative ingredients. Worth a special journey.'
> (Michelin)

There are, of course, problems with international benchmarking services. Firstly, even with a standards checklist, it is difficult to ensure that 'like' data is collected since individual hotels/restaurants in different countries have various assessment and different data collection systems. So, data needs to be treated with care. That is one reason why we often refer to the things we create as performance 'indicators' - they are sometimes imprecise, sometimes flawed but they serve to **indicate** performance and progress. Used wisely such data can form the basis of effective review and improvement strategies.

These systems change over time - and the population of hotels and restaurants covered by such schemes grows over time. Thus, any one particular hotel or restaurant in any country can slip down the rankings simply because a number of possibly newer, higher rated premises have joined the benchmarking club. Thus the data - and the points/stars based on it - need to be scrutinised with care.

However, as 'indicators', such schemes do offer the public some assessment of the 'quality' or 'performance' of particular groups or individual facilities.

3 WHY PERFORMANCE MANAGEMENT FAILS

In Chapter 1 we had a nice, positive introduction to this book ... showing why performance management is important in helping monitor, analyse and improve performance ... and ensure progress is made towards organisational goals and growth.

So, why is this chapter called "Why performance management fails".

Well, unfortunately, it often does. Though many organisations do indeed have performance measurement and management regimes, when questioned about it they often suggest that the value of such a regime is limited.

> The problem with measurement is that it can be a loaded gun - dangerous if misused and at least threatening if pointed in the wrong direction.   (O'Leary 1995)

There is clearly a mismatch between the theory and the practice. We know it should do us good, but often it doesn't.

We need to understand this mismatch. The theory (underlying performance management) is simple and sound. It must therefore be something about the way that the theory is translated into practice that results in 'unacceptable performance' (pun intended!)

Quite rightly over the last couple of decades there has been an emphasis on 'balance' (giving rise to measurement systems such as the Balanced Scorecard) ... based on a recognition that a measurement regime based solely on financial performance misses other important factors.

This identification of causality is one of the benefits claimed for the Balanced Scorecard. When constructing and implementing a Balanced Scorecard, the organisation is expected to identify those actions necessary to drive forward the corporate strategy ... and then to establish performance measures which assess the impact of these actions. These measures form the basis of managerial control and decision-making.

In practice it seems as though - even when using the Balanced Scorecard framework - organisations fail to adequately 'think through' from strategy to actions to measures.

Some of the additions and amendments to the Balanced Scorecard process have attempted to address this issue. The 'strategy map', for example, was devised by Kaplan and Norton themselves (the devisers of the Balanced Scorecard itself) to make explicit these links from overall, corporate strategy to action items under the four perspectives of the Balanced Scorecard (Financial, Customer, Internal Business Processes and Learning & Growth) (Kaplan & Norton, 2000).

Of course this assumes that most business leaders are adept at strategic planning and will take the time and effort to go through a structured process of creating and mapping their strategy. This is rather a large assumption. Of course many managers DO plan ... but whether they do so effectively is open to some doubt.

One might assume that as managers get older, wiser and more experienced they plan better. And perhaps they do. However as Mintzberg suggests there is a difference between strategic planning and strategic thinking.

Those managers who attempt to become wiser as they get older (by subjecting themselves to education, training and development processes) tend to concentrate on planning. They involve themselves in processes that help them analyse, reform and re-arrange but do little to help them synthesise new approaches. (Mintzberg, 1994).

Mintzberg is not suggesting that managers need not plan; only that it is 'necessary but not sufficient' if those managers want to lead their organisations to success. Good planning - if based on the wrong premise, the wrong understanding of the environment, the wrong assessment of competitors - will fail. Mintzberg's view is that managers need to be strategic thinkers before they are strategic planners.

This needs more thought. What is it that managers should be doing to ensure success?

At senior levels, most managers ask 2 fundamental questions on a regular basis.

Answering these questions can be done on the basis of intuition (or perhaps more fairly, by using experience and judgement) or on the basis of (relatively) hard evidence provided by data collected about the situation or process - the part of the plan - under review.

Some would argue that using experience and judgement is 'real' management and is all about 'flying by the seat of your pants' ... eschewing management theory and relying on intuition (Gegax, 2005) Many 'hero-managers' fall into this category - and it is clear that someone with vision and talent can make a success of a business.

"Richard Branson bootstrapped his way from record-shop owner to head of the Virgin empire. Now he's focusing his boundless energy on saving our environment."

Summary profile on the TED website (www.TED.com)

This reflects a common belief that 'real' leaders are born, not made and that 'too much book learning' is counter-productive to effective leadership. 'Real' leaders were practical, non-nonsense, experienced managers or CEOs who seemed to thrive on leadership, and used their charisma, and an approach to leading their businesses which might see them training staff one minute and organising an event the next, to become the dominant personality in 'their' hotel or restaurant.

However, we only hear about the 'hero-managers' who do in fact become heroes, leaving a large number of others trailing as 'zero-managers'. Relying on vision and charisma is not, we believe, a sound choice.

Yet there are lessons to be learnt from these 'special people' and their success. Vision and charisma are useful attributes ... again necessary but not sufficient.

It is not surprising that the hospitality sector has its share of hero-managers, nor that a number of the internationally-recognised hotel chains are named after true leaders and pioneers who created the first such chains. J.W. Marriott, Jr. for example, over 60 years, took the eponymous hotel chain from a family restaurant business to a leading global lodging company with more than 3,700 properties in 74 countries and territories.

Hero-managers are competitive individuals who like to be right and debate issues in ways that make it clear they want to (and will) win. Issues are often 'black and white'. Asking others for advice and help is regarded as a sign of weakness. Too often they narrow down their focus onto the one most important measure - the bottom line. In the hospitality industry a hero-manager might be looking at earnings per share, or other budgetary issues, as opposed to balancing out the measures. After all, satisfied and returning guests are what creates the earnings.

Another problem with hero-managers is that their existence can undermine any devolution of leadership, a deep flaw in a large hospitality business where the 'engine room' of improvement is so often in the hands of the Department Heads and Supervisors, who should be centrally involved in tracking, monitoring and intervening to drive the real improvements in quality service, customer satisfaction and staff performance. If data goes up (or down) the organization and misses out the middle then there will be no improvement.

Roger Smith, of General Motors, used to say, "I look at the bottom line: it tells me what to do."

When Roger Smith became chairman of General Motors in 1981, the company had a 46% share of the US car market. Nine years later when he stepped down, that share had fallen to 35%. By 2007 it was barely 24%. (The Independent, 2007)

Some suggest that hero-managers are effective ... but only particularly so in times of uncertainty. This kind of charismatic leadership can be dysfunctional in times of relative stability, perhaps because it tends to generate unnecessary change (Gill, 2009).

So, it might be a case of "Cometh the time, Cometh the man" but if the time is wrong, perhaps we need less of a hero and more of a thinker.

Roger Smith's concentration on a single measure is perhaps taking 'focus' too far, but it does seem that hero-managers tend to focus on a small number of measures, which 'tell them what to do'.

And there are occasions when concentrating on a single measure might be the thing to do.

Buckingham, in his book "The One Thing You Need to Know" suggests that 'single, controlling insights' do in fact exist in many management and control situations (Buckingham, 2005). He cites an example of this 'one core measure' or 'core score' concept when Sir David Ramsbotham, then chief inspector of Her Majesty's prisons in the UK, was asked what his key measure of success was for the prison system. Sir David explained that during the prison reform process he engineered, he had changed the measure from 'number of escapees ' to 'number of repeat offenders '. This fundamentally changed the values and culture of the prison system and is an example of a leader-driven, 'visionary' approach to performance measurement.

As ever, there must be some kind of 'happy medium'; somewhere between the over-analysis and strategy-driven excesses of 'professional management' and the 'seat of the pants', the 'I know what I know' attitude of some hero-managers.

Our contention is that this 'happy medium' relates to where you focus your measurement.

- ▶ **If you have too many measures you lose focus.**
- ▶ **If you have too few measures you might miss something important.**
- ▶ **If you have the wrong measures you won't retain control.**
- ▶ **If you have measures at the wrong levels, it's too late to exercise control.**

The 'right' measures are the 'key and critical measures' - the 'key indicators' and the subset of 'critical performance indicators', th suggested in Chapter 1 (and will discuss in more detail in the ne that will improve the chances of success and help drive business growth.

(If you already have the right number of appropriate measures, you must have read this book already!)

There is one other, very important factor to consider. One that is mentioned by every management textbook and guide; and one that is frequently overlooked by managers. Communication!

If we have measures … that relate to targets … and we are hoping that this combination of measures and targets will in some way cause behaviours to change … then, clearly, those that we expect to change must know about - and preferably understand - those targets and measures that relate to what they do and what they influence.

In most organisations, communication is considered to be 'bad'; 'poor communication' is cited by most employee focus groups as the thing that most annoys them … and affects their motivation and well-being. This is also true within the hospitality industry. However, we should recognise that 'it was ever thus' … the same results would almost certainly have been obtained from focus groups 20, 40 and even 60 years ago. Kursh, 40 years ago, suggested that 'poor communication' was akin to 'original sin' - a general explanation of the ills of the world (Kursh, 1971).

So, we may not move the 'communication success meter' very far … but we do have to make sure we move it in the right direction insofar as our chosen measures and targets are considered. We may not be regarded as good communicators; but if those who need to know do indeed know what measures relate to them, and what targets relate to those measures, we can be content.

If we are promoting the concept of **key** and **critical** performance indicators, we have to make sure we involve - and engage - the key and critical stakeholders.

We said earlier that communication is mentioned in every management guide and text … yet is often poorly practised. This suggests one of three things:

▶ **That managers don't read the guides provided for them**

▶ **That managers don't believe the advice they are given**

▶ **That managers believe the advice but don't know how to apply it.**

If either of the first two bullet points is correct, there is a massive publishing industry wasting its time. If the last bullet point is correct, there is a massive publishing industry being ineffective.

Our hero-managers are often very good communicators (at least downwards). They know that others need to know what is expected of them.

> John Browett, CEO of Dixon's - the UK electronics retailer - seems to have turned round a struggling company, and done it during a recession (2010-11). His approach?
>
> "Running a good business is all about flat structures and openness. My view is that society has changed and that people expect modern leaders to be close to what is going on. It is the colleagues in the stores and the warehouses who actually deliver the business and we have to make sure we are giving them all **that they need to do that job in the right way.**"

So, we can see that there are some things that might need to be put in place to underpin an effective performance management regime, and we can see that sometimes the nature of organisational leadership has a pronounced impact.

Now sometimes organisations do all of the right things … and they do them well. They rigorously go through a structured process (like the one in this book) and they build a measurement regime which addresses their identified needs. But when they look back a few years later, they still consider the project to have been a failure. Why?

Well, there are two fairly obvious answers. Either:

(a) They only **thought** they had built an appropriate measurement regime which measured the right factors; or

(b) They did indeed build an appropriate measurement regime which measured the right factors ... but they left it in place too long, forgetting that the organisation is organic and its plans and directions change as the environment in which it operates changes ... or as the needs and requirements of customers change. A measurement regime which was once satisfactory may not remain so. Thus any measurement regime, any set of KPIs and CPIs, needs regular review and updating.

Our challenge is to offer information and advice that makes sense; that builds on the positive attributes of hero managers, (focus and clarity), is easily understandable, and can easily be translated into effective, flexible practice. Luckily we can explain our overall aim very simply (and if you can't explain an overall aim very simply, it is probably too complex and should be simplified).

Our aim with this guide is to help you determine - for your hotel, restaurant or hospitality based business:

▶ **what will underpin effective performance and business-wide performance management**

▶ **what the X (right number) and Q (right kind) of measures should be; and**

▶ **how best to communicate those measures throughout the business.**

References

Buckingham, M. (2005)
The One Thing You Need to Know
Free Press

Gegax, T. (2005)
By the Seat of Your Pants; The No-Nonsense Management Guide
Expert Pub

Gill, R. (2009)
Theory and Practice of Leadership
Sage

The Independent 2007
Obituary of Roger Smith
The Independent, 3rd December, 2007

Kaplan, R.S. and Norton, D.P. (2000)
Having trouble with your strategy? Then map it,
Harvard Business Review, pp. 167-176, September-October

Kursh, C.O. (1971)
The Benefits of Poor Communication.
Psychoanalytic Review, 58:189-208

Mintzberg, H. (1994)
The Fall & Rise of Strategic Planning
Harvard Business Review, Jan-Feb

O'Leary, D.S.
Joint Commission on Accreditation of Healthcare Organizations.
"Measurement and Accountability: Taking Careful Aim"
Journal of Quality Improvement 21(July 1995): 354-357.

Ted.com
http://www.ted.com/speakers/richard_branson.html
accessed June 2011

4 WHAT ARE KEY AND CRITICAL PERFORMANCE INDICATORS?

All the most interesting questions result in other questions. This one does too. The first question to ask is "What is really important to our business, be it a hotel, restaurant or other hospitality-focused business?" What drives its success?

Though there might be a number of possible answers to this question, top of the list must be something about enabling every staff member to maximize their potential and through that satisfy every customer. Perhaps 'satisfy' is not the right word, it suggests we aim only to satisfy, but for the purposes of this book, we will expand its meaning. 'Satisfy' will be taken to mean 'delight', ensure their willingness to tell others about their great experience at our property and to return.

This, though, is simply the top of the pyramid - to meet this aim, the hotel, (we will use hotel as an example only), has to do other certain things right. So, developing staff potential to enable them to satisfy customers is the aim ... but not what has to be managed directly. It is these other factors that have to be managed ... because getting these right is what drives this ultimate aim. These secondary factors are the **critical success factors**, the things the hotel must do, and must do well, if it is to achieve its overall mission.

25

The idea of 'success factors' was first raised by Daniel back in 1961 (Daniel, 1961) and the concept has proved popular and resilient. This is understandable - it's a simple concept and it has a 'commonsense' feel about it. "There are certain things that an organisation has to do and has to do well to be successful." Difficult to argue with is, isn't it?

It seems to make sense to 'strategists', to 'planners' and even to our 'seat of the pants', hero-managers.

Of course the management theorists have refined the concept and they talk about a range of different types of critical success factors - industry factors, strategy factors, environment factors, temporal factors, etc. (Rockart & Bullen, 1981). The problem is that, though this kind of further exploration can sometimes help refine ideas to the point where we can understand them better, too often it results in further questions, a wider set of issues and the loss of the inherent simplicity of the original concept. We then 'lose' a number of the people we are trying to influence who want relatively simple messages, simply presented.

So (in the spirit in which this book is written) we intend to keep the concepts simple … and translate those concepts into actions that retain the 'commonsense' feel of the original simple concepts.

A relatively simple definition comes from Bruno & Leidecker (1984) who define CSFs as "those characteristics, conditions or variables that, when properly sustained, maintained or managed, can have a significant impact on the success of a firm competing in a particular industry" but we prefer an even simpler definition.

> CSFs are "those things you have to do - and have to do right - to succeed and develop".

Doing them 'right' almost certainly means doing them better than - or at least as well as - others attempting to do the same things. In a hotel context, the use of the word 'competitor' is not strange. Hotels have to out-sell and compete with other companies.

Policy is driven by competition. In cities, there are many competing hotels. If a hotel has the wrong policy, i.e. no room service after 12-midnight, they might find they have fewer and fewer guests, as the policy of the nearest competitor is a 24-hour room-service. Competition might drive the first hotel to change its policy to 24-hours.

Critical success factors are not the same as key or critical performance indicators. CSFs are the things we have to *do*; KPIs and CPIs measure and quantify our progress towards strategic objectives.

This is so important we ought to repeat it.

> Critical success factors are the things we have to do if we are to be successful.

It is often said when creating a set of key performance indicators (KPIs) that you should focus on outcomes not process. i.e. you should not measure what people do, but what they achieve. However, what people do is perhaps the biggest influence of what they achieve. A salesman who makes no sales calls is unlikely to close many sales. So, when considering critical performance indicators, we might indeed have some process measures - measuring what people are doing, or measuring how long a process was running. In the hospitality industry, we measure the performance of managers and staff through various means, but we can, in part, use observations to assess how well they carry out the process of manage guests/customers, or how they deal with staff issues. Of course those basing their judgements on the indicators we create will use their own knowledge and experience to 'assess' such process factors, and will be aware of the fact that not all actions lead to successful outcomes. They will also be aware, however, that a lack of action rarely leads to successful outcomes.

Each hotel (or restaurant) must identify a small number of these factors that 'have a significant impact on success' ... and that move the hotel forward towards its overall aims in support of the mission.

Some might think that all hotels will have the same critical success factors - after all they all exist with the same underlying purpose. However, not all hotels have the same mission - it depends on the type of hotel it is, (i.e. luxury, standard, budget, city, beach etc.) its geographic and historic context and the type of guests. However, all hotels are measured by the same rating and category accepted within their specific location, i.e. Europe, UK, Asia, Americas or International.

So, the broad mission of maximizing the potential of each staff member to ensure the satisfaction of guests might apply to all hotels - but this may be translated into different specific missions by different hotels - different for city hotels than for those in the country or at the beach; different for luxury and budget hotels. This also means competitors vary resulting in different policies for each type of hotel, its location and the guests it aims to attract.

In determining the mission of a hotel, we would suggest you start with understanding exactly what type of hotel, (or other hospitality business), you are, what type of guests you want to attract, your location, think about national regulations and the changes that are occurring outside of your control (regulatory change, technological change, Food & Hygiene Requirements etc), the rating system in your area and what you aim to achieve for your hotel, (i.e. five or four stars), and then come up with your CSFs ... those things that you have to do - and have to do right - to succeed and develop.

Managing budget is almost always a CSF. For many - if not most - businesses, one or more CSFs will relate to the competition. As we have suggested, this certainly applies to hospitality facilities - almost all are in a competitive marketplace ... both competing against one another and competing against other demands on the wallets and purses of potential customers.

A full set of success factors could be quite extensive and would represent all appropriate levels. However there is a danger in extending the term 'CSF' too far and losing the inherent focus that should result from identifying a small number of **critical** success factors. For example, we have seen some organisations include what we would term 'risk factors' such as the ability to retain key personnel. Clearly such factors can be (very) important but they are not essentially CSFs. True CSFs are much more directly linked to operational processes. For example, if a business is opening a new hotel in a different area, then recruiting an appropriate team might be a critical success factor *for that project*. However, when we use the term CSF, we mean those things that the currently operating business should do - and do well - if it is to succeed and grow. This is not a precise science ... and all organisations must select those CSFs which they think represent their own key factors ... no-one is going to assess how well they have done in arriving at their list. What matters is that the list does indeed represent the critical issues they have to get right.

To help identify critical success factors, we should ask:

What do we want to have happen in this time period if we can concentrate on only a few things?

What would hurt us most if it went wrong?

A simple example might be when a hotel is implementing new process technology - for the front office, for example. Of course all the technical factors have to be addressed, the equipment has to work and be reliable ... but a critical success factor is acceptance of, and understanding of, the system by the staff. Too many organisations concentrate on the former (the technical processes involved) and forget about - or pay lip service to - the latter ... getting the workforce on board.

Even the way in which we write down our CSFs can make a difference ... and can help tell us whether they are indeed critical. We said above that CSFs represent things we have to **do**; we should therefore always try to write using 'action verbs' and we should write clearly and concisely. So, appropriate verbs might be'

- ▶ **Deploy**
- ▶ **Increase**
- ▶ **Implement**
- ▶ **Beat**
- ▶ **Reduce**
- ▶ **Improve**
- ▶ **Deliver**
- ▶ **Accelerate**
- ▶ **Produce.**

Once we have identified our 'success factors' - the things we have to get right - we need to know how well we are doing in relation to these factors ... and whether we are getting better or worse over time?

The success factors must be translated into performance indicators ... those things the business should measure to know it is 'on track', that it is getting the things done that result in the critical success factors looking good!.

These will exist at a number of levels as the 'top level' indicators (representing the whole business or a complete process) are translated into 'tactical' indicators (perhaps representing a specific faculty or department, or a specific sub-process) and into 'operational' indicators (perhaps representing a specific workgroup or a specific support service.) Important indicators of how well we are doing are usually termed Key Performance Indicators. We want, however, to add an additional term - that of critical performance indicators. Key and critical performance indicators are both important components of an effective measurement regime.

All of the things we need to measure are important; otherwise we would not bother to measure them. However, some of these things change relatively slowly over time. If we check them on a weekly, monthly or even longer-term basis, we can assure ourselves that we are on course towards meeting our aims and objectives … in support of our mission. If, for example, we think that training and development of the workforce is an important component of our strategy, we will establish a training/development plan which may map out over 12 months or longer. As long as we check monthly that planned events/developments are taking place, we should be OK. Measuring the development of employees skills, for example waiters at a busy city restaurant, might be a key performance indicator - a good predictor of future performance. Our measurement process must allow us to identify those waiters that have development needs and improve those staff to lift their performance?

However, for some of the factors that affect our success, the timescales are much shorter. … and, when constructing a measurement and review regime, we have to put an additional focus not just on what is important, but on what is 'critical'. We may well have a comprehensive performance management regime with a whole host of (key) measures and indicators, but the CEO/General Manager and the leadership team will first want to know the status of the critical indicators. Others will use the 'less critical' (though no less important - still 'key') measures to support their management processes and to support performance improvement activity.

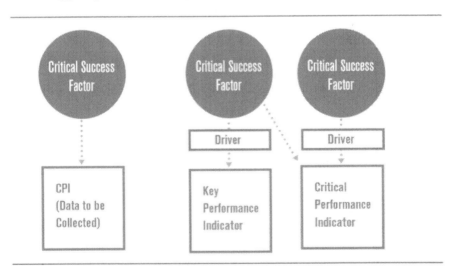

There will not necessarily be a 1-to-1 mapping of key or critical performance indicators to critical success factors. Such a mapping makes things nice and easy but sometimes more than one indicator might have to be applied to a particular success factor ... and sometimes one indicator might furnish information about more than one success factor.

What matters is that each critical success factor is 'covered' - that we have enough information to judge success.

Maskell suggests with specific relation to world class manufacturing organisations that performance measures should have the following attributes.

- ▶ **They are directly related to the manufacturing process**
- ▶ **They primarily use non-financial information**
- ▶ **They vary between locations**
- ▶ **They change over time as needs change**
- ▶ **They are simple and easy to use**
- ▶ **They provide fast feedback to operators**
- ▶ **They are intended to foster improvement.**

(Maskell, 1991)

This suggests that important attributes of a key performance indicator are relevance, flexibility, simplicity, timeliness and ... utility. These attributes apply to the hospitality industry just as much as they do to manufacturing organisations.

Many managers look at the higher level measures ... perhaps on a quarterly or monthly basis and can get a feel for 'progress'. But as we know, these higher level measures are often 'composite' measures ... and if something is wrong, we need to know which component is causing the problem ... we need to know which of the measures at lower levels will tell us this ... and who should have seen this measure and taken action before the poor performance was reflected in the higher level figures. These are the **critical performance indicators** - those that have the NOW factor ... that give us information fast enough to allow us to take action before real or long-term damage is done.

These are the measures that the CEO/General Manager should want on his/her desk on a regular basis to get a 'feel' for how well the hotel/restaurant is doing. These are the measures that our hero-manager - who almost certainly practices MBWA (Management by Walking About) - will ask for as he/she walks around the hotel lounges and restaurants, talking to guests and staff alike, observing practices and solving issues.

> A Chain of Small Lodges decided that its 'reputation' was its key market differentiator and thus monitored performance indicators from external organisations that measured the lodge's reputation. After doing this for 3 years, it realised that monitoring this 'key performance indicator' gave it no opportunities to improve and influence the measure. It had to go back and think through the success factors that drive differentiation and construct some 'lower level' critical performance indicators which could be used to change behaviour and affect its reputation.

In the spirit of making sure our key messages are clear and concise, we now take what we have discussed so far and distil it into a series of 'principles' that apply to key and critical performance indicators. If you 'test' any of your current (key) performance indicators against these principles and find they 'fail', then they are probably not **key** performance indicators.

The Six Principles of Effective Key/Critical Performance Indicators

1. Everyone Knows It Matters

There has to be absolute clarity about the measures and indicators being used. Those who provide the data on the measures, and those that can influence performance in the areas being measured, must know that these measures are key …and are being recorded and reviewed regularly. They should know that the results - as indicated by the measure/indicator - matter.

2. Everyone Knows Who Is Responsible

It should be clear as to who is responsible for the performance against each measure … and this may not always be the obvious individual or team. Key and critical performance indicators must lay the focus (not the blame … as there can be a number of reasons why performance is 'down') on the responsible agents. In most businesses, we are dealing with rational, intelligent beings. However there are still those who might blame their identified under-performance on their staff, managers or even the guests/clients. Part of the process of introducing a comprehensive set of performance indicators must be to help change the culture to one of self-evaluation and self- improvement.

3. Everyone Knows What Is 'Good' And What Is 'Bad'

Measures go up and down … and measures generally relate to targets. When a measure is reported, everyone involved should know whether it represents 'good' or 'bad' performance and preferably how good or how bad. The measure - and/or the way in which it is reported and presented - should convey this information directly and clearly. This also means that the measure/indicator must be responsive to changes in the situation or process under review. Too many measures - used in practice - hardly ever change. This means that those reviewing them stop looking at them with any interest. If the value of the measure does not immediately tell you whether something is 'good' or 'bad' it cannot be a **key** or **critical** performance indicator.

> If you always do what you've always done, you'll always get what you've always got.
>
> Measuring and reporting lets us identify potential change.

4. Measuring And Reporting It Should Change Behaviour/Outcomes

If everyone knows it matters ... they should know this well enough for them to strive for good performance. The very fact that the measure exists - and that people know it exists - should change behaviour.

5. Keep It Simple/Keep It Right

It helps if an indicator is clear, unambiguous and simple. This makes it easier for people to understand it and affect it. In part this stems from getting the other 'principles' right. If an indicator satisfies these other criteria, it probably is simple enough ... but it does no harm to look at whether a proposed indicator can be changed to make it more transparent, and clearer to all concerned ... without, of course, losing its effectiveness.

6. For A Performance Indicator To Be A Critical Performance Indicator, Measuring And Reporting It Should Allow Timely Correction/Improvement Intervention

We referred above to the NOW factor ...we need the information provided by a performance indicator in time to take corrective action before longer-term indicators are affected. Those who are responsible for performance against the indicator should have the knowledge of what action to take and the responsibility for taking such action.

We have seen proponents of performance measurement (and key performance indicators in particular) suggest that proposed measures should be scored against a set of criteria such as these ... to determine which are the 'best' (those that score the highest when rated on each criterion). However, when we are focusing on the really important indicators, such 'scoring' is irrelevant. Each of our KPIs and CPIs must meet all the criteria.

We have - rightly - suggested that a key benefit of having an effective set of KPIs/CPIs is to facilitate business improvement (and the improvement of the various processes that operate within that business). However, there is also something of a 'circular argument' here in that it is always advantageous - and more effective - to measure well-designed processes. If the basic concept of a product or service is faulty, no amount of teamwork or individual effectiveness will save the day … and when you measure a poorly designed process, you will probably get poor results.

> Most of us get really annoyed when telemarketers call us when we are having dinner. The chances of making a sale at that time are almost zero. The marketers assigned to the dinnertime slot should call another time zone or simply rebel … the basic service design does not allow them to be successful.

Level

We can see from the above discussion that CSFs can be expressed at a reasonably 'high' level - but that often as we move towards establishing particularly KPIs/CPIs, we tend to move 'down' the ladder. This is important in that it is essential to translate CSFs and the KPIs/CPIs that arise from them to a level where they can be influenced or controlled. Departmental heads/Supervisors need to know what they have to control to have an influence on KPIs or CPIs that might only indirectly or partially relate to their department. So, when we establish CSFs, we should involve various levels of the workplace in discussions to enable this 'translation' to occur - so that everyone does in the end know what matters - for their job, their role.

Balance

Of course the measures collectively must have some kind of 'balance'; and should reflect the impact of organisational activity on all the major stakeholders. We don't want sub-optimal behavioural change. But equally this balance must be 'real'; it should arrive from a consideration of the critical success factors and the way in which performance impacts on those factors.

If we have the right mix and balance of success factors, we should end up with a well-balanced set of key and critical performance indicators.

Do We Need to Measure the Performance of Individuals?

It is important to co-ordinate group and individual measures ... and to recognise when these things need to be measured.

Performance 'measurement' of individuals is rarely well-handled by organisations; it often reflects antiquated, formal specifications and processes that do not reflect current practices or concerns. If we cannot see how measuring aspects of individual performance affects our KPIs/CPIs then we have a dysfunctional measurement system. Even if we consider introducing performance-related pay, there can be issues. Performance measurement is not a simple process ... and if you get it wrong in ways which allow those being measured to change the measures by game-playing, you do not necessarily get the changes you intended. We suggested that game-playing occurs when those being measured genuinely want to change the measures, but not necessarily their performance. How much more is this true when financial or other gain is involved?.

Availability of Data

We have to be able to know the value of our performance measures/ indicators when we need to know them ... and we will almost certainly have some schedule of regular reporting. This, naturally, means that we have to have a process for collecting the data that forms or helps build the indicators.

If such data is not currently or readily available, then we need to ask questions such as:

Availability: Is data currently available? ... in the right place? (How do we get data from Department Heads/Supervisors to the data crunchers responsible for reporting the aggregated data?)

If not, can the data be collected easily?

Timeliness: Is the data available when it is needed. How frequently must the data be collected and reported to be useful?

Cost: What is the cost of collecting the data?

If these questions cannot be answered satisfactorily, we may have to rethink the indicators we have selected … or use 'proxy' measures or indicators that do exist or can be implemented relatively easily and cost-effectively. The alternative (unfortunately too often seen in practice) is to omit measurements that are difficult to carry out … meaning one or more critical success factors may not be covered.

We referred here to the use of proxy indicators or measures. A proxy measure is a surrogate or substitute indicator used for reasons of cost, complexity or timeliness where we cannot measure the results we want directly.

A Fire & Rescue Service normally devotes considerable resources to fire prevention through inspection, advice, training, etc. How does it know if such activities are useful and cost effective? It cannot measure the number of fires that do not occur because fire prevention processes have worked.

It may, however, be able to compare the numbers of fires - and resulting losses - in a given period to an earlier period before the fire prevention strategy/activity was in place … and infer the number of fires that have been prevented.

Summary

So, we are saying that you should know what is REALLY important to your hotel/restaurant/hospitality business… and we say that this should relate to the guests/clients, their needs and desires, what they think is important.

Then we work through what we need to do - and get right - to deliver on our 'promise to those guests', what we need to do to deliver our mission. We do this on a number of levels throughout the business. These are our critical success factors.

'Traditional' key performance indicators are often regarded as being 'strategic' rather than operational. However, we are arguing here that though all key performance indicators are important (and need to be addressed), some of the performance indicators might well be - indeed should be - operational … because it is these **critical** indicators that give early warning of issues and problems that might not show up in those 'key', strategic indicators for some time.

For each of the critical success factors we ensure that have at least one key or critical performance indicator telling us how well we are doing. We make sure that these performance indicators adhere to the six principles outlined above; we have enough of these indicators to give us a balanced view; and we have data available to populate the indicators. We then filter all of these measures and indicators through our knowledge and experience before making our judgements on the level(s) of performance of (parts of) the business.

We then have a sound basis for control. We know what is important and what is critical … and we know how well (or badly) we are doing against those things we know to be critical.

In the next section ("Getting It Done") we will look at the process we should follow to make sure we deliver on this potentially effective regime of key and critical performance indicators.

References

Bruno, A. & Leidecker, J. 1984

Identifying and Using Critical Success Factors

Long Range Planning, 17 (1)

Daniel, D. R. 1961

Management Information Crisis

Harvard Business review, Sept-Oct 1961

Maskell, B.H. 1991

Performance Measurement for World Class Manufacturing: A Model for American Companies

Productivity Press

Rockart, J. and Bullen, C., 1981

A primer on critical success factors

Center for Information Systems Research Working Paper No 69.

Sloan School of Management, MIT, Cambridge, Massachusetts.

5 BENCHMARKING

When we have measures in place, we use them to judge how well we are doing … for example, by comparing our performance with our planned performance. However, it is also helpful if we can adopt measures that are comparable with those used by other (similar) organisations so that we can compare our performance and have a better indication of whether we are performing 'well' or 'badly'. This process of comparison is known as 'benchmarking'.

Even if we cannot get the information we need to compare ourselves with other similar organisations, we can adopt 'internal' benchmarking - where we compare the performance of one of our processes or departments or divisions against the performance of a similar process, department or division.

However, 'external' benchmarking - where we compare our performance against the same kind of unit in a different, but similar, organisation - is particularly helpful ... especially, where we compare our performance to that of an organisation that is regarded as an exemplar, as 'best in class'.

The aim is to compare performance and, if possible, to compare structures, processes, procedures, relationships, etc so that we know the level and nature of resources that our comparator organisation is using to achieve their level of performance. This (which is much more like a productivity measure) gives us a much more robust comparison than if we only look at 'output' levels.

Alongside this, another aim is to motivate people within our organisation (or part of it) to strive to achieve those same high standards.

The aim is not to 'copy' the benchmark organisations, but to learn from them and to adopt and adapt elements of their organisation only as far as they can fit within our own structure, culture and broad strategy. Thus benchmarking is often a component of a wider improvement process such as business process re-engineering or quality improvement.

We, in the Institute of Productivity, often work at national or regional level as well as working at the level of individual organisations. When a national government - or support agency - is looking across an entire sector, they often want to know:

▶ **What is the overall performance of the sector compared to similar sectors in their competitive countries**

▶ **What is the variation in performance across the sector. i.e. how do the best performing organisations in the sector compare to the worst performing**

▶ **What can they do to bring the worst performers up to the level of the best performers. .. and to bring the overall performance of the sector up to the level of the best performing international competitors.**

For example, a London City hotel would be keen to know how it performs against hotels in other major cities. It might measure its average daily rate and revenue per available room against its chosen competitive set. From the information, it can tell if it is losing or gaining market share. It will also lead it to begin questioning why one location might appeal to guests whilst another does not.

Furthermore, international hotels will also use internal benchmarking to measure the performance of their group in different parts of the world.

A city hotel will also, however, want to benchmark itself against its competitor set of hotels in its home city - this is the set of hotels aiming to meet the needs of a similar set of guests with similar profiles.

Organisational Level Benchmarking

For commercial organisations, benchmarking is often an individual effort (though sometimes sector or employer-led bodies might initiate studies). It can be a costly affair if a hotel, for example, is funding the benchmarking. In the hospitality industry, the various grading/star systems are a simple form of benchmarking - but they rarely offer enough detail to make them useful in terms of identifying ways in which improvements can be made.

Guests (and, importantly, potential guests) may however use such established benchmarks as part of their decision-making process when choosing a hotel or restaurant.

Of course, not all hotel and restaurant proprietors or managers will agree with the criteria for, or the judging that results in, these awards and ratings. They may want to use their own 'better' benchmarking system. They cannot, ignore, these 'public' systems however - since their customers will not.

Benchmarking Agencies and Clubs

In business, trade associations are sometimes helpful in organising and sharing benchmark data across a specific sector or sub-sector.

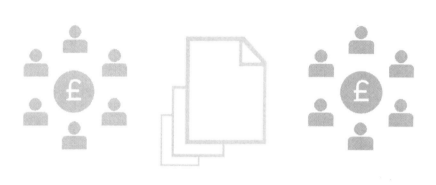

For example, PWC operate a 'Global Best Practices knowledge base' which offers a number of quantitative benchmarking tools to help a company analyse its process performance.

In the UK the Local Authority Performance Benchmarking Club provides members of the Club with a set of Excel based tools which contain comparative information on key performance measures both for outturn performance at the end of each year, and also quarterly in-year data.

Star Global are one of the many independent consultant companies which collects hotel data and sells the benchmarking information onto clients. One of its reports includes the following:

- Property performance against the aggregated performance of a chosen set with the ability to select up to four competitive sets
- Benchmark of up to 18 months of historical occupancy, ADR and RevPAR data
- Year-on-year percentage change, rank and index
- Segmentation data

- Visibility of brand, cluster and regional performance against competitive aggregates
- Identification of hotels that are performing well or underperforming.

Similarly, BSI's Corporate Benchmark Report analyses transactional data to provide an overall picture of performance across industry sectors in both the transient and meetings category, with specific emphasis on the following performance indicators:

• Transient spend and room night consumption by accommodation type

• Changing trends in average stay duration and booking lead times

• Rate variances by star rating/accommodation type

• Year-on-year average room rate performance for core UK & European city hubs

• Policy and programme compliance including online adoption.

This segmenting and categorising of data means that hotels are able to set a variety of indicators - and targets - to reflect their particular priorities and aspirations.

Of course benchmarking organisations charge for such reports and, whether mandatory or optional, raw data from your hotel is required to establish the overall, aggregated performance data and its view of your hotel compared to this aggregated data. However this cost and effort may be significantly less than that involved in trying to establish your own benchmarking operation.

One of the necessary conditions for successful benchmarking is stability in the overall environment - so that over time, 'like' can be compared with 'like'.

Benchmarking data can help the hospitality industry by:

▶ **assisting them in creating realistic and achievable targets**

▶ **stopping them from being complacent (when they think their performance is 'good' but do not know that the performance of other, similar businesses is 'better')**

- ▶ giving them something to aim for in our continuous improvement
- ▶ allowing CEOs/Managers to see what is possible - providing a strong motivator for change
- ▶ helping them identify areas where they are weak … and indicating what might be achieved if they improve.

Reference

Stapenhurst, Tim (2009)
The Benchmarking Book: A How-to Guide to Best Practice for Managers and Practitioners
Elsevier: Oxford

Section 2
GETTING IT DONE

Getting It Done :

INTRODUCTION TO THE CASE STUDY

To help you work through the practical aspects of establishing a successful and effective measurement regime, we are going to use a case study of a hotel in the north of England.

Of course we could have used a restaurant or some other hospitality facility (and we will come back to restaurants later). We decided to use a hotel since they are more complex facilities. However, the principles we will work through apply to any facility, so if you are more interested in restaurants, coffee bars or some other type of establishment, stick with us, the lessons you will learn should be transferrable to your chosen facility.

The JTM is a four star hotel and is the oldest of a small chain of hotels located in the north of the country. Even though the hotel has not been doing very well of late, the Owner/CEO has a 'special relationship' with the JTM, as it was the first hotel he set up and managed. He developed the initial mission for the group of hotels:

We are exceptional operators of contemporary 4 star hotels, creating value in every encounter with our owners, guests and associates.

The Owner/CEO has allowed it not to meet its financial targets for over two years, supporting it with profit from the other nine properties. He realises, however, that this cannot continue and has told the General Manager he must make it work or the hotel will be sold or closed down. The General Manager has six months to show real improvement that is sustainable.

JTM as an individual hotel, has a formal mission statement which is:

To become the leading 4 star hotel of the group by creating a positive and memorable experience for each guest through service that focuses on individual needs in a unique and inspiring atmosphere."

There are 200 rooms in total, comprising:
- 25 junior suites
- 150 single/double rooms
- 25 triple/family rooms

The following table summarises the features of the hotel and the room amenities.

Room Facilities (all rooms include)	Hotel Features
• Clock radio • Complimentary toiletries • Daily housekeeping • Desk • Hair dryer • In-room safe • Iron/ironing board • Private bathroom • Shower only • Wake-up calls • Air conditioning • Climate control • Coffee/tea maker • Complimentary local newspaper • Direct-dial phone • Flat-panel TV • Free wired high-speed Internet • Satellite TV service • Cots available upon request	• Restaurant • Bar • Room Service 24 hours • Small swimming Pool • Small sauna room & splash pool • Gym • Concierge and Business Facilities available • 4 large meetings rooms with presentation equipment • Parking Facilities

The drop in performance in recent times ids exemplified by guest comments on feedback forms which include:

"….the waiter was abrupt. We felt we were in the way…"

"…my room was not made up until 6pm. I had to wait in the lobby for 4 hours without any offer of refreshment…"

"…..the barman ignored me, even though he wasn't busy…"

"…there were no fresh towels provided at the pool. I had to go back to my room to get some and then the attendant told me I was not allowed to use them and took them off me as if I was a thief. I was insulted and will never return to this hotel again."

"...the cashier took ages to calculate our bill, even though we told him we were late for a meeting..."

Of course, once such comments were relatively private or 'contained'. However, nowadays with the availability of 'social' travel sites such as Trip Advisor, such comments are often in the public domain - capable of doing real damage.

6 GETTING IT DONE: ESTABLISHING CRITICAL SUCCESS FACTORS

We now know - in concept - what we mean by critical success factors … and we know that for each of them, we need some form of measure or indicator that tells us how well (or badly) we are doing in relation to that factor. These measures are the key and critical performance indicators.

Collectively the set of measures should tell us how well we are doing against the full set of critical success factors … and, therefore, how likely we are to deliver on our strategy and mission. Additionally the CPIs give us the opportunity to take swift, corrective action to maintain control and increase the chances of the (longer-term) KPIs heading in the right direction.

Now … understanding this in concept is clearly not enough. We need a process that translates that (simple) concept into a working set of critical performance indicators…. We need to start this with a sub-process that established our critical success factors. This is the job of this Chapter!

We are trying throughout this book to be pragmatic … to give real world approaches and solutions. Our pragmatism extends to how we present things. We have tried throughout this book to use relatively simple language. We do have some 'references' to other books and journals but that is simply to show that there are others thinking about these important issues. (You do not have to follow up any of these references ... but you might want to!) We know that sometimes a picture IS worth a thousand words … so before we explain the process of establishing your CSFs and PIs, let's show you a diagram of the complete process (Figure 6-1). Hopefully, this shows its inherent simplicity.

We should point out that though this process is mapped as an (almost) linear process, in practice it is more of an iterative process … and certainly more 'messy'. A number of the steps overlap and inter-relate. So, though there is a basic flow from top to bottom, you will sometimes have to consider two steps at the same time, or go back to a previous step. This is life!

We believe in starting from where we are, not from where we might prefer to be! So, we might be in a hotel where the concepts underlying critical success factors and critical performance indicators are only partially understood.

If so, there is probably a job of 'awareness-raising' to do to bring people up to speed … but this has to be done in a way that is non-threatening and constructive. (There is little sense in pointing out people's ignorance and then expecting them to 'come on board').

The concept will presumably first surface within the leadership team … possibly because one of the team has been to a conference, talked to somebody who has done something similar already or read this book!

They will need to explore the issue to find out if such a project is right for the hotel … at this time. This will depend on the current state of the hotel … and the magnitude of any current problems it may be facing. Establishing PIs is very important but it is best done within a hotel that is moderately stable.

Once the leadership team is convinced they should go ahead, they will presumably want to discuss it with the CEO/Board and/or Owners of the property, to seek their 'buy-in'. This is such an important project that support from the top is essential. Assuming at least one of these people sit on the board and the idea is, therefore, accepted, the GM will probably want to discuss it with middle managers to start the process of awareness-raising. This might be information giving ("we are going to …") rather than consultation since if the leadership team feels it is a useful exercise, they should have the courage of their convictions and declare that the hotel will embark on a project to create a set of PIs.

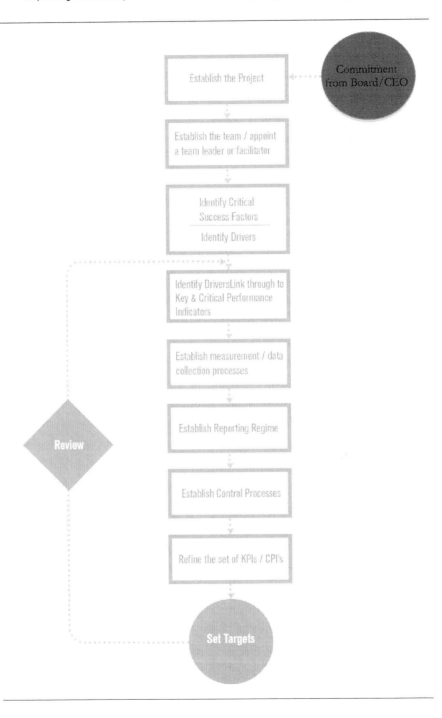

Figure 6-1

Then, of course, they have to turn that simple statement into a working project with a high likelihood of success. They have to start 'getting it done' … by working through a process something like the one in the diagram above.

Now, let's work our way through the process in a little more detail.

We are going to base our process on the diagram … but will fill in details as we go to turn this into a practical set of steps that you can follow when working through your own project.

Step 1: Establish the Project

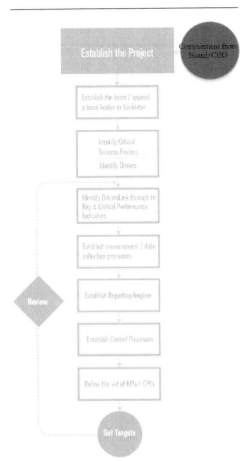

It might sound a bit stupid to say you have to establish the project ... but you do. It needs to be launched so that those who will come into contact with it know that it is important ...

... and if it is important (which it is!) it must have backing from the senior leadership team and the board ... who collectively are the people that have brought the project into being.

They must commit - and must be seen to commit ... and one of them should take overall responsibility. This may be - perhaps should be - the GM ... but certainly there needs to be a designated Champion - the person with the authority to make things happen and to remove barriers in the way.

Executive commitment is often cited as an important factor for project success (in any kind of project). It is often cited because it really is that important. We have used the phrase "what is REALLY important" when discussing the critical nature of some success factors and some performance indicators.

This is REALLY important because creating and using a system of PIs will:

- ► 'touch' all parts of the organisation
- ► impact on the ability of the senior leadership team to plan, to evaluate, to take decisions.

Clearly they have to be committed to deliver on the project and have to be seen to be committed to it. Staff within a hotel soon get to find out what is really important to the senior team ... by the way they talk and act.

So, if you want to create effective PIs as a means of helping you develop the hotel, commit! ...

.... and show that commitment in what you say and what you do.

.

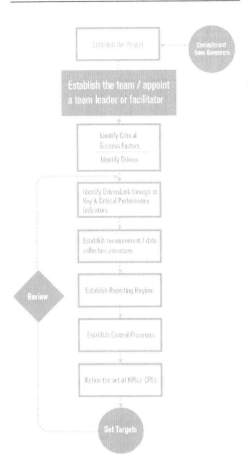

Key and Critical performance indicators must cover all key aspects of the hotel's activities and may cut across specific business processes ... and parts of the hotel structure. This means that a team approach to establishing and implementing the measurement regime is needed ... a genuine team approach with shared, collective responsibility.

The team should have an appropriate mix of knowledge and experience (especially if the PIs are likely to include 'technical' measures) but should be small enough to remain coherent and focused ... probably about 6 is the maximum number. (Additional members with specific expertise can be co-opted as necessary.)

Step 2: Create the Team

It may be that 1 or 2 of the senior leadership members are part of the team, or even a board member, especially if they have experience of performance management from their (other) business life.

Members of the team should be supported by their line managers and should be given the 'time and space' to undertake the role properly.

The team needs a team leader or facilitator ... and he/she must have an appropriate level of authority. This might be 'borrowed' from the PI

Champion - the member of the executive team who has taken overall responsibility for (but not necessarily day-to-day control of) the project. Some hotels have an individual responsible for collecting statistical data - this person could be the team leader, but might be better as an advisor to the team, perhaps with the Deputy GM taking the team leader/facilitator role.

The facilitator is the person responsible for day-to-day activity, for building the team, for communication with stakeholders, for reporting to the champion.

The facilitator/leader requires knowledge of performance measurement concepts and practice ... but also (and perhaps more importantly) needs experience of team-building and project management skills. If the project is delayed, the whole concept of PIs starts to lose credibility, so the project must be delivered to schedule.

Clearly this person is key to success. He/she must have the trust of (and normally be a member of) the senior leadership team.

Obviously in any particular hotel it might be impossible to find a potential facilitator who has all of the required skills and experience. In these cases especially (but in most cases anyway) it is wise to think about appointing an external adviser/consultant who can 'fill in the gaps' of knowledge and experience.

An external advisor will bring in real experience of implementation and might be able to 'short-circuit' some of the phases of the project. Clearly the internal facilitator needs to work effectively with any external advisor and the project champion must take a keen interest in ensuring that there is mutual trust and respect between these two key individuals.

The external advisor is just that - an advisor. The hotel itself must be clear about what it expects to achieve ... the advisor is there to help with the 'how'. The consultant must not be seen (by the leadership team) as an 'excuse' for 'taking their eye off the ball'. ("We have employed an expert ... let's let him/her get on with it!")

Step 3: Identify Critical Success Factors

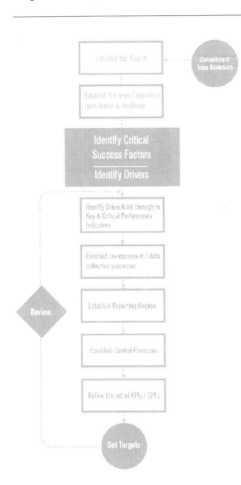

This sounds simple, doesn't it? However, if you get this wrong, the whole project fails.

So, it is vital that you work through a process that ensures you get it right … as 'right' as you can.

We are going to give you a process that has worked in the past in a number of organisations. You can take this as a 'template' and modify it if you feel it needs to change to fit your business.

Hold a 'Kick-Off' Event

The team has to start working together.

Everyone in the hotel has to understand this project matters.

.

These two statements mean that there should be some kind of relatively high profile event that serves those two purposes

We have found that it is important to hold an early PI workshop. Note we use the term 'workshop', not 'meeting'. The team comes together (if only as a set of individuals in the first place) but is expected to participate and contribute. It should be structured but relatively informal.

One of the reasons we use the term 'facilitator' for our internal team leader is because he/she needs to make such an event work ... to draw people into the activities, the thinking, the decision-making.

Such an event gives the opportunity to establish the level of awareness of the underlying topics ... and, indeed, to extend that awareness across the team, so that all share the same 'message'. It is vital that all members of the team share an understanding of the importance of 'getting it right', of creating an effective set of PIs.

It is particularly important that all involved understand the 'principles' underlying PIs that we set out in Chapter 4. This is best done not by 'lecturing' or 'preaching' but by introducing the principles and then exploring what they mean in practice in discussions which use examples from the hotel itself.

Identify appropriate legislative and regulatory factors and any third party standards or benchmarks that could be helpful

Generally your success factors will be important because you have decided they are ... because they determine whether you are meeting the needs and aspirations of your community (and other stakeholders). Sometimes, however they will be important because someone else says they are - the government, Michelin, WTTC, Eurohoteliers or some other body.

So, it is important that you are aware of any legislation or regulation that you must comply with.

There are, of course, various kinds of standards, best practice guidelines and benchmarks that might offer a useful framework for development. If you decide to adopt one (or more) of these frameworks, there will be obvious implications for the factors you will have to measure.

Write the Headline

This workshop can explore the mission, strategy ... and, crucially, the critical success factors for the hotel.

What defines 'good' and what do we have to do to achieve it?

One useful way of taking this discussion forward is to ask those present to write a headline representing what might be said if the hotel was taking part in an Awards ceremony.

This helps the group think about the issues that are worthy of report in a very small eulogy ... a headline. Some of the points made should lead the group towards the critical success factors.

From Mission to CSFs

Once you have got people thinking about 'good' and 'bad', 'success' and 'failure' ... add a little more structure.

- Write down the hotel's mission and main strategic goals on a flipchart - so that they are clearly visible to the group
- 'Brainstorm' success factors - the things the hotel has to get right to be successful in moving towards these goals and this mission. (If discussion flags, you can introduce key areas in which CSFs might occur - quality, quantity, time, etc.) Make sure you are discussing issues (factors) that underpin those things the guests and/or stakeholders are looking for from you. (In this case, although the guest is paramount, the stakeholders might include the owner/shareholders, board, senior leadership team and/or suppliers.)
- The minimum output here from the brainstorming is a statement such as:

... and we would probably be looking to arrive at a list of something like 6 or 7 items.

It is difficult not to include a whole list of factors - especially the 'motherhood and apple pie' factors such as 'achieving guest satisfaction' or 'recruiting excellent staff'. These phrases are applicable to all hospitality businesses, but are too general. Here, the team must go at least one step beyond this level of thinking - to identify those things the hotel needs to do well in order to achieve guest satisfaction or recruit good staff.

Discuss whether each of your potential success factors is really important - what would happen if you were 'off target' or slightly out of control. How much would that matter? Would it 'reach' particular stakeholders? What would the guests think? What might stakeholders do?

For the ones that are (still) considered to be (potentially) critical success factors... discuss them in more detail. Talk about success/failure. What would be different between the two states? How would you know (without measuring)? When would you know? When would the guests notice? How would they notice? Would the owners/shareholders and stakeholders care? How much?

Decide which of this short list are truly critical. (This question cannot be asked too often!)

Of course, by this process you identify whether each of your potential critical success factors is really that - a CRITICAL success factor.

When you are satisfied that each of your factors does 'pass the test', you then have to take a look at the complete set of (draft) CSFs and ....

Check for completeness. Are you missing anything?

As CSFs are identified, an attempt should also be made to understand the drivers (internal and external) that shape and impact upon these CSFs. These are the things that cause the CSF to change. You need to know what it is that moves you in the right direction ... and what might occur to throw the proverbial 'spanner in the works'. The list of CSFs can be categorised ... and even, perhaps, grouped or combined, so that we know those that are subject to common drivers. For example, we might have a set of drivers related to Equipment or Skills or ….

This categorisation will depend on the nature of the planning and review process being undertaken: it might be according to the stakeholders group(s) affected; to the processes involved in the measurement or to the specific strategic aims being impacted. By categorising, you might see linkages, overlaps and duplications that allow you to cut the overall number of critical success factors - always a good thing (as long as you maintain comprehensive coverage of all key areas).

The eventual list should be examined and challenged to make sure these CSFs are indeed 'critical'. There should be some way of ensuring that when you say 'critical', you mean critical to underpinning guest requirements for example. They might also be CSFs linked to gaining a Michelin star or passing a local Food Safety and Hygiene Standard in the kitchens.

In an ideal world, you would test your CSFs with the stakeholders they are aimed at, i.e. the guest, the owner, an external testing body. Focus groups, one on one meetings or surveys could be used. Finally, the CSFs must be presented to and/or approved by, (dependent upon level of autonomy), the executive leaders and board.

Cure the GM!

As the team moves towards an understanding of what really matters, set this scenario. The GM is ill. He/she is off work for 1 month, unable to take the slightest interest in what is happening. When he/she returns, what will he/she want to know - first? What questions will he/she ask? If your early prototype CSFs don't match up with the answers to these questions, they are probably not CSFs.

At the end of the meeting you should have (at least a first draft) list of CSFs. If you don't … you will probably need a supplementary workshop after people have had time to reflect and discuss things outside of the 'formal' workshop. This is not a 'race' … you need to do it effectively rather than do it quickly. Once this draft set of CSFs is produced, the team leader/facilitator should take it to the project champion for a 'go/no go' decision on taking the next step.

Presumably if this is a 'no go' there is some refining to do. This must involve the team (and not just the facilitator) because they must agree to the final set of CSFs … as this is the basis for their next phase of work.

This is a conversation the JTM General Manager had with his Rooms Division Manager, (who is also his Deputy GM), and the Food & Beverage Mgr:

GM:　　We need to show clearly through precise measures that we are improving. We already have the advantage of a great location.

F&B Mgr:　I agree, but what exact measures does the owner want to see?

RD Mgr:　Obviously financial, but there are other important measures too, such as number of covers in the restaurants and how much is spent per guest on food & beverage. That is how we add value and profit.

F&B Mgr:　That isn't wholly true. The number of rooms occupied affects covers, but also how fast the rooms are turned round and the number of return guests, or even guest complaints are just as important.

RD Mgr:　We need to be able to measure outcomes; complaints, as a financial measurement, are not easy to apply. The owner wants to see growth within six months. The restaurants are easier as they have an immediate effect on the bottom line.

F&B Mgr: I disagree. You're talking about quick fixes only, not sustainable concepts....there are much more important measures if we are to become competitive, such as benchmarking against local hotels.

GM: Arguing is not getting us anywhere. I think the first thing to do is to form a team to decide what is important to us; what if we didn't do it would result in our closure. Focusing on our critical success factors will allow us to set up measurements.

This next phase of work - which moves you nearer to your final set of PIs - is outlined in the next Chapter.

We heard earlier that the mission of JTM is …

"To become the leading 4 star hotel of the group by creating a positive and memorable experience for each guest through service that focuses on individual needs in a unique and inspiring atmosphere."

Whether this is a 'good' mission is irrelevant … many business have mission statements that are 'motherhood and apple pie' but this mission does give JTM something to aim at.

JTM has indeed established a programme to use performance measurement as the basis of improving what they do and how they do it in order to improve the overall performance (and the sustainability of that performance), and ultimately, avoid a sell-off or, worse, closure.

The Owner has decided the GM should lead this project as it is vital, although the GM may have the Deputy GM manage the day-to-day tasks. The Deputy GM is also the Rooms Division Manager, although he has a highly competent assistant who can take over some of his duties during this time.

This means the GM is the 'performance champion'. In consultation with the Deputy GM and the Department/Sub Department Heads - it has also been decided to create a project team - lead by the Deputy GM (CDM). The project team consists of the F&B Manager, Housekeeping Manager, Kitchen

Head Chef, Restaurants Manager, HR Manager and Regional Manager, (who also sits on the board for all hotels in the group), 7 people in all.

Their job is to propose a performance measurement and management process together with a set of appropriate key performance indicators which can underpin progress in meeting the hotel's mission.

If they are following our methodology, they would first establish the project and introduce it to staff. The owner, regional manager or general manager, (or even all three together), might present this to staff to show it truly has their backing and that staff are expected to pull together and make it work. In the case of JTM they have an additional motive of not wanting to lose their jobs if the hotel is closed down.

The next step is to determine their critical success factors. They must know what it is that they must do - and do well - to be successful and achieve their mission.

Clearly these CSFs must relate to the key factors in their mission … and because of the nature of JTM's current position, it should relate to factors other than 'simple' examination of performance.

It is not unusual for companies to have multi-factor, broad mission statements - but a very limited set of critical success factors. This suggests that the 'motherhood and apple pie' mission is simply 'window dressing' - and does not reflect the true - and deeper - values of the hotel.

However, in our case, JTM needs to address both the mission and the wider needs of the business. A meeting of the performance project team was held and after iteration (over a period of 2 weeks) with the leadership team, a set of critical success factors was agreed.. (Remember the CSFs are nor the ultimate aim - they are what has to be done to achieve that ultimate aim.)

Critical Success Factors

These critical success factors are to:

1) Improve profitability by winning new and retaining old customers
2) Improve the quality and consistency of service to guests in all areas, but especially restaurants
3) Improve the overall offer with new or extended products/services, (i.e. weddings, free WiFi, evening entertainment, external gym membership)
4) Exploit new technologies that can support management information, customer profiling & relationship building, and benchmarking
5) Develop staff at all levels to improve standards, increase productivity and reduce waste
6) Show sustainability of progress by establishing new processes and procedures to embed the development of growth, building relationships with the customer and the hotel as a place we are proud to work in.

These CSFs recognise the need to address all customer and stakeholder needs, as well as some of the issues that have come up in the last twelve months in the customer surveys, comments made by AA and staff. Perhaps Department Heads can become involved by holding focus groups with their teams, or setting up an anonymous suggestion/issue box.

Visits to competitors prior to the CSF meeting assisted JTM in understanding what they needed to do to win and retain customers, although more work in this area needs to be done. JTM now recognises that there are, in fact, underpinning elements necessary to secure strong performance and move towards JTM's wider mission. Of course, different hotels might identify the same or similar CSFs but in a different context because of their own current state of development. Improvement for one hotel might be renovating rooms, whilst for another, it might be changing a system. There might also be genuine progress targets that aim to seek excellence in one or more of its areas, i.e. fine dining or fastest turnaround of rooms.

7 GETTING IT DONE: ESTABLISHING KEY AND CRITICAL PERFORMANCE INDICATORS

So, you have your team, your champion and perhaps an external facilitator - and they between them, and in consultation with principal stakeholders, have arrived at a set of critical success factors. These must still be regarded as provisional until we are sure we can create appropriate performance indicators that represent each of them.

(When identifying CSFs it is sometimes very useful to think about the 'drivers' - the things that cause the factors to change because when it comes to identifying/creating suitable measures, sometimes it is more important to measure the change in driver factors rather than in the CSF itself. This acts as a kind of 'early warning', recognising change before it has 'rippled through' to change the CSF value.)

So, you now need a process to take these CSFs and drivers ... and transform them into a set of key and critical performance indicators. As before, we will use our diagram of the full process - but add some detail - to take you through such a process.

This is another job for the (same) team. Hopefully they are now more of a coherent team; they have worked together on identifying CSFs and they understand the principles that underlie effective PIs.

(Of course we are also assuming that, if the team has not been working effectively as a team, the team leader/facilitator - and the external advisor if there is one - will have taken some action to remedy the situation. Such actions are outside the scope of this short book ... but there is no shortage of books on team building!)

The next phase of the project calls for another meeting or workshop. This one should be easier since the group is already a working entity ... the barriers to communication and participation should already be down ... and people should feel happy about contributing and having their contribution recognised.

We know that we need a mix of key and critical performance indicators. Key indicators are just that ... key to judging our performance, our well-being, our progress on one or more of our critical success factors. Critical performance indicators are also key performance indicators but have the 'added value' of measuring short-term results and effects which serve to give us early warning of problems and, more importantly, the opportunity to take corrective action before too much damage is done.

If we are measuring 'operational' factors, there is good chance that we will be able to identify critical performance indicators. For others, perhaps environmental factors (such as energy usage if that is important) we may also be able to identify CPIs. For other factors, and especially for social and behavioural factors, we will probably have to be content with key performance indicators - no less important, but not as urgent.

Step 4: Link from CSFs to K/CPIs

Get the group to list all the things that **could be** counted, measured or assessed and would tell you something about the CSF/driver. For each of these, get the group to give it a 'High', Medium' or 'Low' score dependent on how well it would help you understand good/bad, success/failure/in control/out of control for the CSF ..

… and ask them to score it 'High', Medium' or 'Low' in terms of how feasible it would be to count, measure or assess it.

The scores are only to make the team think about the issues … but they do give a useful summary of the 'level of feeling' … and can therefore help shape the final view of a particular indicator.

This process of working through possible measures and moving to a focus on probable measures is helpful for hotels in conducting the self-evaluation of performance, particular against criteria established by, say, the head office of a group of hotels or external bodies such as WTTC Carbon Measurement Initiative.

This discussion should lead to a much richer understanding of the issues involved in the measurement process … and should lead to a shortlist of PIs for further, more detailed analysis.

The PIs identified or created should be comprehensive - covering all of the CSFs and/or drivers of those CSFs.

For each item suggested as a PI, the following questions should be asked:

▶ **Which CSF(s) or drivers does it relate to?**

▶ **Could it be combined with, or represented by, a simpler measure?**

▶ **Who would use it?**

▶ **How would they use it?**

Sometimes these questions cannot be fully answered without moving onto the next step ... so steps 4 and 5 are usually done together.

Step 5: Identify How Measurement Will Be Made

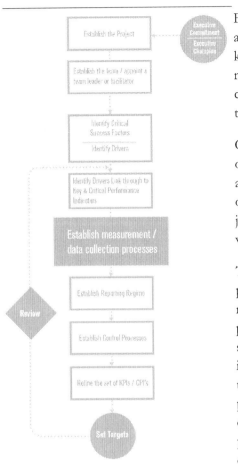

For each of our PIs, we must have a data collection process ... so we know what the value of the measure is ... and this data collection process must give us timely data.

Collecting data (rather than relying on feelings and instincts) mean we are working with 'facts' rather than opinions. It is always easier to justify subsequent decision-making when it is based on 'hard' evidence.

The first set of data we collect is particularly important. It is a measure of the 'baseline' performance level - where we have started from. This is the information we need to measure the success of any improvement projects we initiate ... by comparing the 'after the project' performance date with this baseline data.

For some PIs, it may not be possible to collect 'hard', quantitative data. For example, measuring customer satisfaction is often done by questionnaires, surveys and focus groups. Though this is 'soft', more qualitative data, we still need to ensure we follow a reliable, structured process to gather the data - a process that can be repeated so that we can subsequently get comparable data.

Wherever possible, for obvious reasons of convenience and cost, we will use data which is already available - perhaps collected for another purpose. (But remember that you must not distort the measure(s) you intend to use just so you can use already-available data.) Clearly, though, it is helpful to use those data sources we referred to earlier - where we have reliable, comparable data provided by third party agencies. Where this is not the case, a specific data collection process must be established and tested.

In Chapter 3, we also raised the possibility of using proxy indicators or measures where the data collection process is just too difficult or too expensive. (A proxy measure is a surrogate or substitute indicator used for reasons of cost, complexity or timeliness where we cannot measure the results we want directly.)

When thinking about data, it is important to remember the "3 R's" that represent the characteristics of 'good' data. Data should be:

▶ **Reliable - it is credible and consistent; the processes by which we manipulate/calculate the data are accurate and consistent over time**

▶ **Relevant - it clearly relates to the critical success factor it is designed to help us understand**

▶ **Representative - it is typical of the process/function/activity being measured.**

So, the job of the team is to work through another set of questions.

▶ **Where is the data that supports our desired PI? What is the source of this data we have to collect?**

▶ **Does the data already exist? If not, how can it be collected/recorded?**

▶ **Who is or should be responsible for collecting the data?**

▶ **What is an appropriate measurement frequency? (When do we need to know? How often might it change significantly?)**

We need to work through these issues and questions until we are confident that we can establish processes that will furnish the data we need to present or build each of our PIs.

This process of establishing the links between critical success factors, the drivers of those success factors and the eventual key and critical performance indicators and the data we need to make it all usable is often best done diagrammatically. A 'picture' of these linkages is much more succinct and transparent than any text could be.

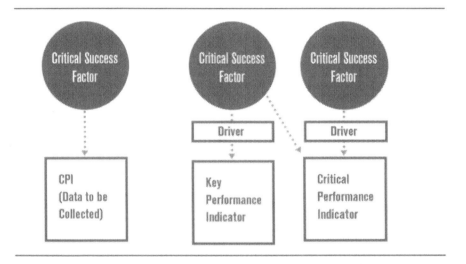

Of course we need to ensure that we have covered everything that is important - so we need to go back to our strategy and to our CSFs to ensure we have a balanced set of measures that do not:

▶ over-emphasise any part of our operation or any part of our strategy

▶ miss any important part of our operation or strategy.

It is worth creating a table to summarise your selected KPIs and CPIs so that you can see at a glance whether you are covering all of your key strategy factors. Here is such a table for a manufacturing organisation keen to address all of the SEE (Social, Environmental and Economic) factors. (We will see a similar example for JTM later.)

Indicator	KPI?	CPI?	S	E(nv)	E(con)
Labour hours per tonne	Yes	Yes			X
Energy costs per tonne	Yes	Yes		X	X
Litres of water per tonne	Yes	Yes		X	X
% of suppliers ISO14001 registered	Yes	No		X	
No of reportable accidents	Yes	No	X		
No of employees volunteering	Yes	No	X		

We are getting there. We now have a set of CSFs and a draft set of KPIs and CPIs that link to them. The next chapter adds a vital component to this 'mix'.

We know what we are trying to achieve at JTM and we have a team working to establish a performance measurement regime which can drive improvement. We have a set of critical success factors and we are now in the process of linking through to appropriate performance indicators.

Our critical success factors are:

1) Improve profitability by winning new and retaining old customers
2) Improve the quality and consistency of service to guests in all areas but including restaurants
3) Improve the overall offer with new or extended products/services, (i.e. weddings, free WiFi, evening entertainment, external gym membership)
4) Exploit new technologies that can support management information, customer profiling & relationship building and benchmarking
5) Develop staff at all levels to improve standards, increase productivity and reduce waste
6) Show sustainability of progress by establishing new processes and procedures to embed the development of growth, building relationships with the customer and the hotel as a place we are proud to work in.

Example - CSF 4

Let us take a look at one of these to illustrate the process we have been through in this chapter. We will take the 4th CSF about the use of technology.

What are the drivers of this factor - the things that will cause it to change?

In their workshop, the project group decided that possible drivers were:

▶ The quality of the JTM's IT infrastructure - including the availability of hardware/software support

▶ The technical skills of the staff using the equipment and software, and their ability to analyse data resulting from it

▶ The availability of IT hardware and software to meet the needs of the improvement activity

▶ The penetration of computer use throughout the hotel.

So, the group started to look at things which would tell them how well the hotel was doing in relation to the main CSF or these possible driver.

Suggestions were:

1. Number of computer training courses/days attended by staff
2. Number of computers staff had access to
3. Number of logons to the hotel network by staff
4. Number of staff able to use data to carry out specific tasks - such as building or updating the customer database, strengthening customer relationships.

Linking Measures to Strategy

This factor is a useful reminder that measures link to strategy and strategy links to measures. Within the overall development plan for JTM, there is a specific plan to implement a new management software system - and JTM has decided to adopt 'Guest-Point Software' - a well-established, user-friendly programme developed specifically for smaller hotels.

The project to implement and adopt Guest-Point Software is at a very early stage but is regarded as a key part of the development plan. A few staff have been trained as 'early adopters'. The hotel realises that using all the elements of the programme competently may take up to a year, but wants to see evidence of progress quickly and assess how it benefits the hotel and guests.

Example Two

For further illustration, we will also see how the group have worked through the establishment of indicators for CSF1 - relating to 'improve profitability by winning new and retaining old customers'.

The project team brainstormed some of the detailed performance indicators they would expect to underpin this, splitting them into two areas: management and customer care. Their brainstorming elicited the suggestions for measures shown in Fig 7-1. Some of these potential measures were actually considered to be more relevant to some of the other CSFs. (This is typical of brainstorming which is a 'messy' process.... The key is to capture all ideas and then subsequently decide where they might have some advantage.)

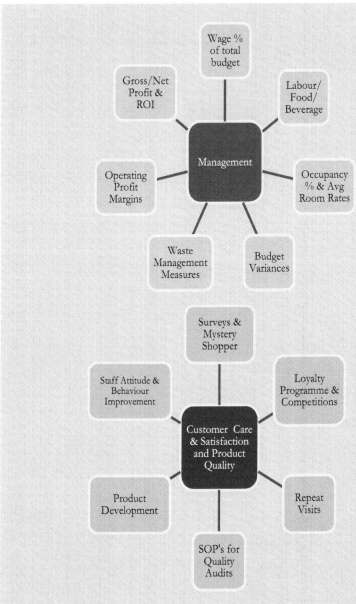

Fig 7.1

This process leads to the following proposed key performance indicators to underpin CSF 1.

	Performance Indicator(s) – CSF1
1	Monthly gross profit compared to previous year at same time
2	% increase in guest numbers
3	% of returning guests

The last CSF incorporates one of the most difficult elements to quantify. How we measure 'proud to work for' is tough. In general we all know what feeling proud of something is, yet how would you measure it in a workplace setting. Could staff absenteeism or lateness be an indicator? Does it make a difference to guest satisfaction if staff are proud of where they work? Are standards higher because of it?

However, often an imperfect indicator that helps measure progress against a particular CSF is better than no measure. Of course, the hotel could undertake an annual or 6 monthly staff questionnaire and directly ask the question about whether they feel proud to work for the hotel - but they are much more interested in seeing the effects of any such pride and loyalty - improved staff engagement and initiative, fewer customer complaints about staff, and so on .... so they decide to build some of their KPIs under CSF6 against these (slightly) more direct factors.

Slowly by taking each CSF in turn, the team inches towards a list of performance indicators they feel can effectively measure progress on each CSF and therefore of the overall mission.

These KPIs, after discussion and clarification, are then agreed by the board as a means of measuring 'process' and 'outcomes' that reflect the hotel's priorities in pursuit of its mission.

There is some debate in performance management circles about whether process measures are true measures at all. Some suggest that measuring what you do - rather than what you achieve - lets people 'off the hook'. However others suggest that for any factors - especially those with long timescales and those that are multi-faceted - it is not practical to wait for outcomes and then measure them. It is then too late if the outcomes are not what you anticipated. They also argue that if a strategy and action plan is rational and designed to underpin achievement, then measuring the progress of that action plan is a necessary function in itself - if we do not complete the planned actions, we are unlikely to achieve the planned outcomes.

Establishing the full set of CPIs and KPIs is an iterative exercise, involving consultation and discussion with all key stakeholders. A full list of performance indicators for JTM, underpinning all of the CSFs and arising from such a process, is shown in the next Chapter.

8 GETTING IT DONE: REPORTING

Step 6: Establish Reporting Regime

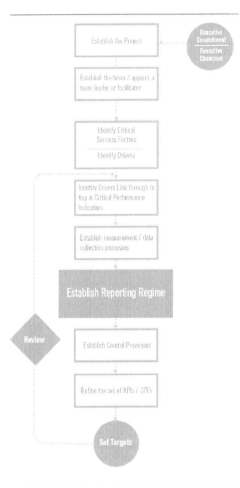

We must establish reporting mechanisms for each indicator ... and for the set of indicators, making sure that those who need to use the data get that data when, where and how they need it.

Since the purpose of measurement is to help control and to make improvement happen, the normal frequency of reporting of a standard performance measurement programme depends on how often it is appropriate to intervene in the process under review.

The control or improvement action could be anything from simply escalating the reporting of the indicator level to a higher tier of management through making specific adjustments to the technical parameters of a process to establishing an in-depth analysis/improvement project.

On our diagram, we have the next step in the process (step 7) as 'Establish Control Processes'. In practice, these two steps - 6 and 7 - are often considered together as they are inter-dependent. Control can only be effective if those responsible for control action receive data in a timely fashion and in a form that makes the data clear and useful.

On a factory floor, measures might be taken every minute because the particular machine might be capable of near instantaneous adjustment. The individual members of a family of measures - at factory floor level - might be summarised and reviewed on a daily basis and the balanced family might be reviewed weekly.

At departmental or divisional levels, individual measures might be made and reviewed weekly, and the balanced family reviewed every two weeks or monthly.

At senior, organisational levels, some individual measures would probably be taken no more than monthly with the aggregated set of measures reviewed less frequently - perhaps quarterly at board meetings. In exceptional cases, for specific projects, measurement might be more frequent - say, weekly - but generally major corporate programmes cannot afford that many checkpoints.

In a hotel context, measurement and control at a managerial level on a daily basis is unlikely - though, of course it will take place at the supervisor level, and the daily and weekly activities that take place in a hotel will all affect the KPIs. Of course where we have specific projects being implemented or where we have particular initiatives in place, control will be 'stronger' and more frequent. Thus, in a situation as dire as JTMs, a morning meeting might review the figures, and a weekly meeting might lead to control and change measures. However, it is probable that at a monthly meeting, more measured plans for control and change would be made.

Of the KPIs in our list, only the staff 'behavioural' indicators could be considered 'critical performance indicators' in that we can take action to change what we do - and hopefully change the measures - if we report frequently and take action based on the figures - especially, of course, where they are different than the expected or target figures. So, although the KPIs for behaviour are expressed in monthly terms, the data manager calculates a rolling 4 week figures for each of these indicators and reports on that figure on a weekly basis.

One of the measures JTM decides to report on is the number of logons to the new system each month - and this seems to be a 'reasonable' timeframe against which to make a judgment about whether and how the new Guest Point Software is being used. However, the number of logons on its own is a 'process' measure - it tells the CEO nothing about what happens during those logons... sometimes it is difficult to get 'measures' for the ways in which things like systems are used … but at the various supervisory and management meetings staff can be asked to provide anecdotal evidence of usage - the way in which they use it … and their feelings on its usefulness … and ease of use.

Of course, some of those things that might be regarded as 'external' performance indicators - such as hotel ratings - will only be published annually. This means that those issues that contribute to such external measures must be monitored in other ways so that the hotel can have a chance to influence the measure.

KPIs often have to be 'translated' into sub-measures and indicators that operate at different levels, or in different departments. Board members want to know the KPIs and that they have been achieved, or why they weren't achieved … but the CEO and leadership team will have a range of other indicators they use to maintain hotel standards and to ensure the business is on track to achieve targets.

So, where a manufacturing organization might have four main reporting frequencies:

- ▶ **real time (or near real time);**   ) **for**
- ▶ **daily;**   ) **CPIs**
- ▶ **weekly; and**   ) **for**
- ▶ **monthly**   ) **KPIs**

… a hotel is more likely to report:
- ▶ **weekly**
- ▶ **monthly**
- ▶ **quarterly**
- ▶ **annually**

…as appropriate for each KPI.

However, annual reporting is not very helpful in terms of ensuring we take the appropriate actions to try and ensure we meet target performance - and this is a case where we may have to switch to reporting on the drivers of the PI - and using those as the effective PI. Department heads would normally collect data on performance - based on achievement/non-achievement of predictions. These figures are then reported and the 'forecast performance' compared to our proposed target is composed. This data can be reported perhaps quarterly, although in the case of a crisis such as JTM, it might be demanded weekly or even daily based on various changes or functions taking place in the hotel.

A reporting regime/cycle for JTM might look like that expressed in the table on the following page.

CSF		Performance Indicator(s)	Reporting
1	1	Monthly gross profit (as a ratio to that of the same month in the previous year)	Monthly
1	2	% of increase in guests	Monthly - compared to previous year at same time
1	3	% of returning guests	Monthly - compared to previous year at same time
2, 5 & 6	4	Number of guest complaints	Weekly/Monthly & Annual figures compared to previous year at the same time - for each area of hotel operation
2, 5 & 6	5	Guest satisfaction (from survey)	Monthly - compared to previous year at same time
2, 5 & 6	6	Number of process reviews undertaken and number of Standard Operating Procedures - SOPs - established or reviewed	6-monthly
2, 5 & 6	7	Number of Quality Audits undertaken (based on compliance with SOPs) and 'passed'	Monthly
3 & 6	8	Number of new/extended guest services introduced within the last 6 months	6-monthly
3 & 6	9	Number (and value) of functions	Monthly

4	10	Number of logons to the hotel network by staff	Monthly
4	11	Number of staff able to use data to carry out specific tasks – such as building or updating the customer database, strengthening customer relationships	6-monthly
5	12	Number of training hours for staff	Monthly
5	13	Number of improvement suggestions made by staff	monthly

So here we have 13 indicators. Hopefully you can see that though some indicators may not be useful on their own, the collective set of indicators should give JTM a comprehensive and balanced view of their performance in terms of accomplishing the critical success factors they have deemed important in achieving their mission.

Level and Trend

The data collected, its frequency of presentation and the form of presentation should be enough for stakeholders to be able to establish both level (what is the current value of the particular indicator) and trend (is it moving up or down … signifying better or worse performance … and is this movement consistent). It is no use looking at an 'improvement' in the indicator and thinking "We are doing well" if the longer-term trend is downward.

If the trend is downward, then we know we have problems to solve. Conversely, if the trend is upwards it doesn't just mean that all is well … it also means that we might have greater scope for improved performance than we had previously forecast.

All of the data collection and reporting processes need to be tested - to demonstrate that they do actually work … in terms of collecting information accurately and in a timely fashion … and in terms of presenting it in a form that is useful to those that have to make judgments and take decisions/ actions based on the indicators.

Where possible, the indicators should be tested with real data … first backward (if possible) and then forward. If the measures are fairly standard, it might be possible to go back in time and put real historical data into the measures and see if it would have been helpful in offering new insights, missed first time around (this is backward testing).

Backward Testing

It is also useful to have a 'run-in' period to assess what kind of interpretation problems might crop up (forward testing).

Forward Testing

So, the results might be viewed as 'tentative' for the first few cycles and the family of measures/indicators might be fine-tuned in this period.

Assuming our set of KPIs makes it through our testing, we should now be relatively confident that we have the basis of a measurement/assessment regime that:

- ▶ **Ensures we meet all legislative and regulatory requirements**
- ▶ **Covers all of the factors we have identified as important**
- ▶ **Will tell us how well we are doing in making progress towards our strategic goals**
- ▶ **Is practical and feasible.**

Dashboards

Performance dashboards/executive dashboards have become popular over recent years. They present performance data in easily accessible/readable formats ... perhaps as traffic light indicators (where 'problem' indicators - those whose value is below or above a 'trigger limit' - are shown in red) or as dials, bar graphs, etc.

The (very sensible) aim is to show a lot of information simply and to allow managers to concentrate on 'management by exception'.

NO WORRIES   TIME TO PANIC

However there are advantages and disadvantages to such forms of reporting. The advantages are clear but such highly aggregated displays can:

- ▶ **over-simplify ... and lead to less discriminating judgement from those reading the data;**
- ▶ **fail to show trends ... and many performance indicators only deliver their true value when they are charted and presented as a time-series.**

JTM has established a set of KPIs and the hotel's data manager has been exploring appropriate ways of presenting the data to make it easy to assimilate and understand.

In a normal situation, a hotel might request reports on a quarterly basis, but time is of the essence in a crisis situation and JTM needs to change quickly. Most indicators are therefore collected or calculated monthly, with a summary report annually.

9 GETTING IT DONE: CONTROL ACTIONS

Step 7: Establish Control Processes

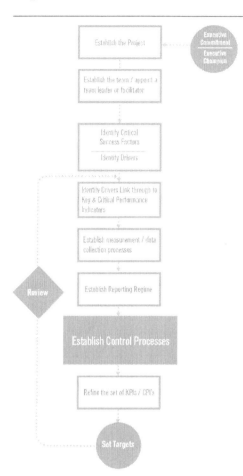

Its crunch time. We are establishing PIs so that we can take - and remain in -control; so that we can take swift, positive action to recover from any fault or problem.

So we have to decide on what kind of action should be taken (and by whom) if any of our indicators show we are off target.

So the team has to determine trigger points and identify the actions to be taken when those trigger points are reached.

One of the main purposes of creating PIs - and especially CPIs - is so that we can take control or corrective action when things are not going to plan. We have also said that we expect our PIs - by their very existence - to change behaviour.

Therefore each of our measures should be capable of being the cause of fast, responsive action to correct any deviation from plan. Yet, of course, any such corrective action must not be sub-optimal ... changing the value of one measure positively but having a negative impact on other measures ... unless we are clear that the positive change outweighs any negative change.

(Another purpose of adopting PIs is to facilitate longer-term, improvement actions. We shall talk about this in the next Chapter ... but, as before, this seemingly linear process might actually be compressed into fewer parallel stages … and, as we talk about control actions, we might also be thinking about the longer-term improvement actions inherent in step 9.)

For any CPI the corrective action should be pre-programmed.

If this alarm goes off, do this.

If the quality level drops below X%, do this.

Of course, the 'control action' might simply be to escalate the situation; to report to 'someone in authority' that one of the indicators has passed a trigger point. It might mean observing the process closely for the next 15 minutes. But it might mean stopping a machine or an entire production line or sounding an alarm. In either case it must be clear as to:

▶ **What the level of the indicator is that triggers the action**

▶ **What the action is**

▶ **Who takes it**

▶ **When they take it.**

The triggers must be set so that any 'alarm' is real - something is wrong! The last thing we want is lots of triggers being activated when only minor faults (which can and should be picked up by the 'operator') have occurred. Too many alarms results in those alarms being ignored … and when we get a 'real' problem situation, that is likely to be ignored also.

Of course in our example we have few CPIs - the only indicator we suggested should be treated as CPI (because early intervention is helpful) is that related to reducing guest complaints, (which needs to be immediately actioned). This is, of course, why we decided to report on this weekly.

However, even here we are not in the industrial machine-based setting where control actions are simple and fairly obvious. This is especially true where - as here - PIs relate to the behaviours of individuals and groups of people …. people do not behave with predictability and do not necessarily respond to intervention in ways we expect. This does not mean that we should not pre-plan control actions, just that we probably need to think about a range of possible actions that can be 'tailored' and 'tweaked' when we need to respond to an 'alarm signal'.

So, if we are having a higher than expected level of customer complaints, we might first want to think about possible causes … and base our control action on that identification. We might, though, have a range of possible actions as potential responses - everything from toughening up the policing, through to special meetings, one-on-one discussions with individuals concerned and even through to the implementation of positive rewards to replace negative sanctions. In the end, any JTM staff member absolutely refusing to come on board would have to be dismissed.

What we do need to be clear about is who is responsible for recognising the 'alarm' and taking any action. In a large industrial organisation, we would normally suggest that such recognition and response is best taken as low as possible in the organisation - this normally results in faster action and the action is then also taken by those with the greatest opportunity to influence 'first level' behaviours. This 'principle' is best maintained within the hotel environment - such that 'attitude managers' (whoever they may be in the hotel hierarchy, possibly at supervisory level) immediately respond to 'poor performance' indicators when observed or if there is a guest complaint.

For 6-monthly indicators where we do not get results for a lengthier period of time, we may have to set our control actions based on the 'drivers' of performance. Thus, if we have a target performance, we would normally collect data on intermediate performance-based on the assessment of ongoing results and timed predictions. These figures would be reported and the forecast performance compared to our proposed target. Where there is a significant difference, again an 'alarm' might be generated and a response initiated before the 6-month period has ended - perhaps a call for supervisory staff to pay particular attention to staff interaction with the guests on a daily basis.

JTM has attempted to set up a fairly robust system for collecting assessment data and using it to create predicted results. This data is aggregated into charts showing levels of progress.

Here is a part of the data table submitted to the CEO and board.

KPI	Target	Board Meeting		
		Month 2	Month 4	Month 6
Reduce Guest Complaints	Fewer than 10	14	11	9
Increase Number of Returning Guests	25%	7%	15%	25%

At each of their monthly meetings, the Board would see the data and would get a report on actions taken in response to the data.

The report format above is simple and clear. The data manager at JTM has experimented with other forms of reporting and, for a while, created a 'dashboard' for the board, which attempted to show data clearly in 'speedometer' form. However, managers simply found this distracting and confusing - and preferred the 'plain numbers'.

Irrespective of the form of display, JTM now has a set of CSFs (and drivers), a set of PIs which enable them to know how well they are doing in relation to those CSFs, and a set of actions, triggered by levels of the PIs to take to make sure they stay on track in relation to those CSFs. Are they finished? Well, almost. First they need to test and confirm that what they have created will actually work in practice.

Step 8: Test What You Have Created

We have to evaluate and refine the individual PIs ... and the collective set of PIs. This is so important; we cannot afford to get it wrong. If we do (get it wrong) we think we are in control, but we are not.

At this stage, it is worth documenting the PIs in some detail ... both to serve as 'the record' but also as the basis of a final examination.

So, we ...

Complete a Performance Indicator Record Sheet For Each Indicator

Figure 9-1 shows a Record Sheet for the KPI relating to improvement suggestions made by staff. These sheets are a useful way of summarising all the decisions you have taken about each indicator, its reporting frequency, what should happen when it shows things are 'wrong' and so on.

Documenting the indicators in this way makes them 'real' .... there is a record of the indicator, how it is constructed and how the data will be used.

Anyone looking at the set of records would be able to see the key and critical performance indicators that have been selected ... and should be able to understand why.

(Incidentally if we have done our job right, that reader should have a very good understanding of our strategic priorities ... because what we measure indicates what we believe is important.)

For the collective set of PIs, you should ask:

1. Do individual measures complement, or conflict with, each other?

2. Does the set of measures provide timely, balanced information useful for control and decision-making?

3. Are any CSFs/drivers not covered?

4. What is the best way of presenting - and disseminating - the overall set of PI data?

5. What are the risks associated with using this particular set of measures? What might we miss? What might we over-focus on?

This sheet also shows us that the reporting process can be a little more sophisticated than simply 'counting' the factors under review. Data is often collected daily, aggregated on a weekly basis and then posted to a monthly control chart, which clearly shows whether the target figure has been exceeded - and clearly shows the trend in the data. (See Figure 9-2) (Eventually, this could be looked at annually.) Interestingly, the target figure may be different for each month for performance indicators where experience of past patterns of behaviour change. Some might argue that for 'negative indicators' (such as number of complaints), any figure is unacceptable -we are striving for 'perfection' and 'no defects' after all. However, JTM have taken a pragmatic view that they live in a world where perfection is unlikely and constant striving for improvement (rather than constant bemoaning of failure to achieve that perfection) is the most pragmatic approach.

Department	Pastoral
Title of Indicator	Number of improvement suggestions made by staff
If it is not clear from the title of the indicator, what actually gets measured/calculated to provide the data for this indicator?	
Person completing this form	Anthony Garside
Date	18th April 2014
Critical success factor(s) which this indicator relates to	Develop staff at all levels to improve standards, increase productivity and reduce waste
Owner (Person responsible for implementing the indicator)	F&B Manager in partnership with RD Manager
User (Person responsible for acting on the data)	Supervisors
What is the source of the data for the indicator?	Staff suggestion box plus suggestions made in team briefing meetings
Could (should) the data be obtained in any other way?	No - this is a direct measure and the simplest means of collecting the data
How often should the data be collected?	At the end of each week.
Is the reporting process/format clear?	Yes – Supervisors provide weekly records to the F&B/RD Mgrs who prepare the weekly and monthly measures.
Does reporting help the user understand level and trend?	Yes - each weekly/monthly measure is placed on a 'control chart' showing all the figures for the current hotel bi-annually.
Does reporting help the user understand actual versus target performance?	Yes - the control chart includes a target figure for each month
Are actions prescribed for different levels of the indicator?	Not fully prescribed but a set of potential actions/interventions has been agreed – but some discretion is allowed.
Is the use of this indicator a cost effective way of maintaining control/progress?	Yes - the simple process involves little cost
Review date	Quarterly

Figure 9-1

It is the breaching of a target (or specific threshold levels for the indicator) that normally triggers consideration of control actions. In a normal situation where a company is striving to improve performance, breaching a target for two consecutive months might trigger an investigation of possible reasons/causes. However, JTM has decided on a policy of 'zero tolerance' and initiates such an investigation as any target is missed.

KPI 13	September				October				November			
	Wk 1	Wk 2	Wk 3	Wk 4	Wk 1	Wk 2	Wk 3	Wk 4	Wk 1	Wk 2	Wk 3	Wk 4
Target	20	20	20	20	30	30	30	30	30	30	30	30
Actual	10	12	11	14	22	25	28	27	27	29	31	33

Figure 9-2

The target was changed from 20 per week to 30 per week in October because JTM had run a number of briefing/training sessions for staff on how to identify improvement opportunities (including how to identify waste) and on the preferred format of suggestions. Understandably, they expected this to make a difference to the number of suggestions they received.

When JTM finished a similar process to record all their KPIs, they subjected them to a final review against the criteria for KPIs.

> Everyone knows it matters
>
> Everyone knows who is responsible
>
> Everyone knows what is 'good' and what is 'bad'
>
> Measuring and reporting it should allow timely correction/improvement intervention
>
> Measuring and reporting it should change behaviour/outcomes
>
> Keep it simple/Keep it right

This is obviously an iterative process. The team worked through these questions a number of times until they answered all of these evaluation questions satisfactorily. They then presented the set of KPIs to JTM's Board and explained the reasoning behind them. After a set of questions to seek clarification and challenge some of the reasoning, the KPIs were accepted by the Board.

Take the CEO Test

However before the team presented to the Board, they did what we always recommend when creating a performance measurement and management regime - they took the Board test.

In any business, the Board has to be convinced that this set of measures will tell them what they need to know to 'get a feel for' the business. In this case, the aim is to see sustainable improvement in specific areas within six months, but, importantly, overall.

Do the CPIs relate to the kinds of questions the GM would normally ask on a Monday morning? If not, do they improve upon the GM's Monday morning questions?

Do the KPIs provide information on the kinds of issues that are standard items on the agenda of the regular leadership team meetings?

If the team - and the GM, (and then the board) - 'sign off' the set of PIs as meeting the need for control, we have got the PIs we need. We have not yet finished, however. Right at the start of this book, we suggested that PIs are instrumental in creating success and growth. This needs more than simple control. The next Chapter takes us on to fulfilling the real potential of PIs.

10 GETTING IT DONE: SETTING TARGETS & BENCHMARKS

Step 8: Targets & Benchmarks

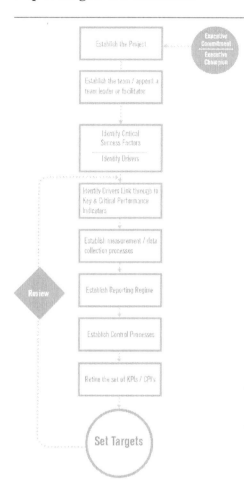

For each of your key and critical performance indicators, you need to establish targets/benchmarks that reflect 'success' ... and perhaps others that represent 'failure'.

When you select a measure or indicator that you think is helpful, you obviously need to know the kinds of results that show you are doing well ... and those that show you are doing badly.

For each of your critical performance indicators, you should establish a target or benchmark that represents 'compliance' - processes are on track and no corrective action is required.

The 'failure level benchmarks' might be the 'trigger points' we talked about in the last Chapter.

These are sometimes called 'critical limits' because going beyond them - in a negative sense - means our performance is unacceptable and critical decisions/actions might have to follow.

Setting targets is not a job for the PI team - or at least not in isolation. Those involved in the work being measured must be involved in the target-setting.

This phase of the project might therefore be taken on by the leadership team themselves ... and/or might be delegated to the PI project facilitator to work with the various department heads to bring forward suggested targets.

We will almost certainly set targets based on a combination of past performance and expectations/aspirations arising from the strategy/planning process. However, if possible we might also set targets based on external benchmarking ... using some of the data we talked about earlier (such as that from Star Global).

The advantage of using an external benchmark as the basis of a target is that it has some credibility. Using a target that can be considered 'challenging' also avoids a business from being accused of 'coasting'.

Even if we do not have benchmark data available, if we are basing targets on known, current levels of performance (because we are measuring them), again we have a basis for credibility and acceptability. We may have to wait until we get a 'feeling' for current levels, and the amount of variation inherent in the process ... but setting up indicators does provide the platform for realistic target setting.

The reasoning behind the targets should be clear and transparent ... we should know what difference achievement of the targets means to the organisation.

In the early 2000s, the UK government established a policy that 50% of all children should progress from school to higher education. The policy was very clear ... but the reasoning was not. The result? A distortion of standards and underfunding that have led to massive, unintended consequences for UK HE.

All targets should be clear, quantified and time-bound. i.e. we should know what we aim to do and by when.

So ... the target:

To ship at least 90% of orders within 3 days of receiving the order

.. is a valid aim ... but not a valid target, since from reading this target we do not know whether the organisation intends to achieve this level of performance in the next week, the next 3 months or the next 3 years.

Goals and targets might compete and conflict. A campaign to reach one goal might impact negatively on the achievement of another.

It is the routine and systematic integration of improvement trends with benchmarked levels that prevents ad hoc, sub-optimisation where one specific target is 'chased' harder than others (perhaps because those doing the chasing think that this is the one that really matters) or perhaps achievement against one of the targets is rewarded more highly or more clearly.

All goals and targets must be 'owned' by someone - an individual, a team or a department. They must be the ones that have the greatest influence on whether or not the target can be met. The PI measures the performance of their part of the process.

Usually, those responsible are 'rewarded' in some way if performance targets are achieved. This may not be a financial reward - it might simply be some form of recognition or praise ('Team of the week'). However, when a group or family of measures is involved, reward and recognition should come not from achieving success against one measure - but, wherever possible, against a number of measures in the family.

After all, if all the measures in the family are key/critical performance measures, we do not want rewards to go to behaviour and performance that cause one measure to be maximised at the expense of other critical measures.

One particular issue is that critical performance indicators can take precedence over (longer-term) key performance indicators ... because the 'urgency' is sometimes taken as a reflection of greater importance. However all the indicators are key indicators and it is up to the leadership team to ensure that the key indicators are not overrun by the critical indicators.

This is therefore a 'balancing act' requiring the weighing of different issues ... and it requires judgement ... almost certainly the judgement of the leadership team and especially the GM. However after the list of (draft) targets is established, the leadership team now has to take control and take responsibility for finalising the set of longer-term targets... that link through to the overall mission and strategy ... and are designed to deliver success.

We have just about completed our process. We have in place:

► **Critical Success Factors (and drivers)**

► **Key and Critical Performance Indicators**

► **Control triggers and control actions**

► **Longer term success/growth targets.**

There are now a couple of important issues to explain and clear up. Stick with us - there are still lessons to be learned.

To recap....

The hotel group mission of JTM is:

For the group of hotels:

"We are exceptional operators of contemporary 4 star hotels, creating value in every encounter with our owners, guests and associates."

JTM's formal mission statement is:

"To become the leading 4 star hotel of the group by creating a positive and memorable experience for each guest through service that focuses on individual needs in a unique and inspiring atmosphere."

To achieve this mission, JTM believe they have to:

1) Improve profitability by winning new and retaining old customers
2) Improve the quality and consistency of service to guests in all areas, but especially restaurants
3) Improve the overall offer with new or extended products/services, (i.e. weddings, free WiFi, evening entertainment, external gym membership)

4) Exploit new technologies that can support management information, customer profiling & relationship building, and benchmarking

5) Develop staff at all levels to improve standards, increase productivity and reduce waste

6) Show sustainability of progress by establishing new processes and procedures to embed the development of growth, building relationships with the customer and the hotel as a place we are proud to work in.

To understand how well they were achieving these factors, JTM (after considering both the CSFs and the drivers of those factors) decided to measure the following:

CSF		Performance Indicator(s)
1	1	Monthly gross profit (as a ratio to that of the same month in the previous year)
1	2	% of increase in guests
1	3	% of returning guests
2, 5 & 6	4	Number of guest complaints
2, 5 & 6	5	Guest satisfaction (from survey)
2, 5 & 6	6	Number of process reviews undertaken and number of Standard Operating Procedures - SOPs - established or reviewed
2, 5 & 6	7	Number of Quality Audits undertaken (based on compliance with SOPs) and 'passed'
3 & 6	8	Number of new/extended guest services introduced within the last 6 months
3 & 6	9	Number (and value) of functions

4	10	Number of logons to the hotel network by staff
4	11	Number of staff able to use data to carry out specific tasks - such as building or updating the customer database, strengthening customer relationships
5	12	Number of training hours for staff
5	13	Number of improvement suggestions made by staff

The leadership team then went on to set targets for each of the KPIs - and for some of them also established 'control limits' that represent the boundaries of acceptable performance.

However, in part the real work starts now. Of course, over time the GM and the Board Members will want to see the figures improving ...and the targets for subsequent years revised upwards. This means that the leadership team has to establish an 'action plan' to bring about such improvements.

This is the 'hotel development plan' - a rolling 3 year plan of activity which is updated annually.

What the performance measurement system has done is to make it very clear to everyone in the hotel what 'success' means and it enables those searching for improvement to understand whether or not they are moving in the right direction.

It also enables the leadership team to talk to departmental heads, supervisors and others about their role in 'moving the figures' and even to establish sub-targets for sub-divisions of the hotel, i.e. housekeeping and health club.

At departmental meetings, those sub-targets and the PIs themselves can be used to illustrate progress (or lack of it).

If we take CSF 1 as an example....

1) **Improve profitability by winning new and retaining old customers**

This clearly has particular relevance to the sales and marketing departments. Both are expected to have an action plan to show how they are addressing the kinds of improvements that will contribute to progress in this area. Because their contribution is so important, a member of the leadership team has been assigned a 'leadership' or 'coordinating' role.

Following discussions with the Marketing Department Head a broad strategy has been approved - and the Marketing Department Head will work with the Sales team to turn this into a detailed action plan.

The strategy includes a number of 'intervention areas', suggesting that the action plan, when produced, should address:

▶ Sourcing of an accurate hotel benchmarking consultant, to benchmark competitors - both locally and internationally

▶ Setting up Mystery Shoppers, Guest Comment Forms and Guest Focus Groups

▶ The creation of new packages for weddings & honeymooners, groups, hiring out rooms and the use of the health club

▶ Working with the F&B Department on the creation and promotion of new menus and offers for the restaurant and bars

▶ The use of the internet for sales and reservations

The Head of Marketing has only 2 weeks in which to report back with an agreed, shared action plan to be implemented over the next 6 months.

It is this use of the performance measurement system and target setting process to drive improvement planning that justifies what can be a significant amount of effort to build and maintain the measurement and reporting system. However it does mean that improvement actions are based on real evidence of current performance, hopefully compared to external benchmarks of competitors and it does mean the resulting action plans are structured and coordinated to address the critical success factors that underpin JTM's mission.

11 How does all this work in a restaurant?

Whether we are running a hotel, restaurant, museum, café or whatever ... the principles are the same. We have to establish our mission and then work from this to determine the critical success factors and then the performance indicators we should adopt to we know we are achieving 'success' against these success factors and striving positively to achieve our mission. Of course, the actual CPIs and KPIs would be different (though clearly some of them would apply to the restaurant activity within a hotel).

The best way to look at this - and to take us forward to further practical detail - is to look at another case study ... this time, of a restaurant.

Darren Carter and Paul Mills have worked in the pub/restaurant trade for a long time - both started as waiters but have progressed, Darren in the drinks side in pubs and clubs, and Paul in restaurants. They are both approaching 40 years old and, after a lot of soul searching, have decided to set up their own restaurant. They seriously considered taking a franchise on a national brand but decided if they were going 'on their own' they would rather stand or fall on their own efforts and abilities. They pooled their savings and borrowed from friends and the bank to purchase an existing not-too-successful restaurant called Emily's in Alwoodley, Leeds, chosen because it has some (though limited) parking available and is close to residential areas with other eating establishments in the area (creating drive past potential customers) but none offering the planned menu for Darren & Paul's venture. Emily's was considered an inappropriate name for the new venture and the décor was in need of a 'refresh' so the restaurant was closed for 3 months while it underwent that refresh to emerge as *the foodery*. It has now been open for 6 months.

Darren essentially runs the bar/cellar while Paul runs the restaurant. They have teamed up with a young, ambitious chef - Kenneth Nolan - who also wanted to branch out on his own but could not afford the investment. He has come on board for a relatively modest salary and a future 10% share in the business if certain targets are met and he stays with the business for at least 3 years.

The immediate mission for *the foodery* is simply survival but Darren & Paul are aiming that it should become known, in the next 3 years, as 'one of the best restaurants in North Leeds' with a reputation for 'wholesome though slightly quirky' menus and excellent service. They see the menus as attracting diners and excellent service as making them return. Thus Critical Success Factors (CSFs) for *the foodery* are:

1. Effective promotion and marketing to ensure a steady stream of first-time customers
2. Selecting and preparing menu items which are attractive to diners but considered slightly 'unusual' or 'out of the ordinary'
3. Controlling costs to ensure reliable and consistent gross profit

4. Creating a positive, consistent customer experience that relates to quality, service, value and encourages customers to stay (and consume) and return

5. Attracting, and meeting the needs of, higher per visit spend customers

6. Developing staff that can deliver all of the above.

After surviving the whirlwind of preparation and opening, Darren and Paul want to take stock of performance and decide whether their 'recipe' for the restaurant is the right one. They want to know where they can improve. They also know that they need information as the basis of identifying those areas for improvement.

They have taken advice from their accountant and from a food sector consultant they employed to oversee the setup of the restaurant and have been advised to establish the following key performance indicators - many of which are commonly used in the restaurant trade.

KPI	Addressing CSF
Food Revenue per customer	2,4,5
Drinks revenue per customer	4,5
Gross profit on bar sales	3,5
Revenue per available seat hour	4,5
Wage costs as a percentage of revenue	3
Food costs as a percentage of food sales	3
Kitchen labour hours per week	3
Kitchen linen costs	3
Sick days taken	3,6
Best (and worst) selling menu items	2,5
Number of press/social media mentions	1,4
Number of advance bookings for the next month	1,4
Customer satisfaction	2,4,6
Staff development points earned for the month (see text below)	6

They are aware that there other things which could be considered important (such as food inventory levels, purchase prices of ingredients, and so on), but they think they have a good balance of measures to underpin achievement of their critical success factors and see them through this important initial stage of operation.

All of these are reported on monthly but Kenneth, the chef, analyses the best and worst selling menu items at least weekly so that he can make sure he has enough of the right ingredients to meet the demand for the top sellers. Additionally, where possible, he uses the ingredients intended for the worst selling items as the basis of the 'quirky' daily specials.

However, this set of formal key performance indicators is not the total extent of performance measurement and management. Their consultant right at the start pointed out that some things are important - but perhaps difficult to measure ... at least on a formal, quantitative basis. Wherever possible, Darren and Paul have tried to identify such issues and address them.

The figures reported so far suggest that customers are particularly pleased with the quality of the staff and the service they deliver. Darren and Paul are particularly pleased with this as they have been working hard to identify – and deliver - what their customers want from *the foodery*. Paul, in particular has been concentrating on ensuring that all customers get a prompt and warm welcome ... and ensuring that he knows the names, and the preferences, of his regular customers. All restaurant staff are trained to offer a welcome - and if Paul is not available, they know that the target is to offer such a welcome within 20 seconds of a customer entering the restaurant. When a table is not available and customers wait in the bar area, Darren and his team know they must update customers approximately every 10 minutes on the availability of their table.

Both Darren and Paul have been junior staff in the catering trade and know that often they were treated as 'disposable resources'. In *the foodery*, they took a conscious decision to both train and trust their staff - forgoing a command & control culture ("do this because I say so") to one of explaining why decisions are taken and trusting staff to react accordingly. They offer initial training to all staff but after staff complete an initial 6-month probationary period (the point that some of their staff are just reaching) they are offered a range of additional training/development opportunities on a voluntary basis. Each training course or development opportunity carries a points tariff and when staff reach a set level of points awarded, they will get a modest salary increase. All staff get a monthly 'performance chat' designed as much to recognise and reward good performance as it is to identify and correct poor performance.

One member of staff with a particular interest in technology and the use of social media has been designated 'mentions monitor' to identify the level and type of online comments made by customers. This 'unsolicited' customer feedback has already been useful in identifying areas that needed improvement (the cleanliness of the toilets being one example).

What Darren and Paul do not have is comparable data from other nearby restaurants (benchmark data), but they do get some information on how customers view and value these competitors both from talking to their customers and through monitoring online comments. Though this is 'anecdotal evidence' it does offer some insight into the relative standing of *the foodery* in the area.

Pause

Though this is not 'an assignment', take some time to think through whether Darren & Paul have put together an effective set of key performance indicators, bearing in mind their CSFs and their simple, underlying mission. Then think how that set of indicators might change over time as *the foodery* gets established or as external conditions change.

We will look further at *the foodery* in the next Chapter.

---

12 Performance Improvement

This book is designed to bring about performance improvement. We know that the single most effective way of doing this is to measure those factors that define and underpin success and then to set targets for moving those measures in the right direction. This is what we have been doing with the process outlined in the preceding chapters.

However, sometimes, 'external' help is required - to create new ideas, new ways of working and so on that become part of the action planning to move those measures.

So, we adopt specific improvement methodologies, tools and techniques - things that have been proven to work across a number of sectors.

Throughout the book, we have been trying to emphasise the importance of understanding your customers and doing those things which offer them additional value.

In the Lean methodology, one of the most important approaches to improving productivity and performance, value is 'king'. Lean emphasises the creation of value above all else. Value is taken to be any attribute of the product and surrounding service that the customer thinks is important and is willing to pay for. Any activity that does not add value in the eyes of the customer is regarded as 'waste' and should be eliminated.

Even 'value' needs a little explanation.

Suppose you are looking to buy a carton of milk and you are at an equal distance from your local convenience store and your local supermarket. You know that the milk is cheaper at the supermarket. Where will you make your purchase?

Factors such as 'good service' used to be regarded as 'value adding' factors - but now these are regarded as being part of the core offering, mere 'hygiene factors' expected by customers from all of the retail (and hospitality) establishments they use. Particularly memorable service might be an added value factor but this has to be more than competent service.

Your decision may depend on other factors such as whether you are in a hurry and know that if you go to the supermarket you will have to queue at the checkout simply to buy one carton of milk. You decide to accept the premium charged by the convenience store for your own convenience. You have taken a decision as to which offers the better 'value' in your current situation. Value is certainly not always about price.

Waiting in a queue is not seen as adding 'value' - and is therefore 'waste'. Restaurateurs try to change the 'queuing' (for a table) experience into one of pleasure and added value by providing a pleasant location (usually a bar) and disguising the fact that you are waiting. However, this works for a limited time period; many customers will move from pleasantly distracted to mildly irritated to annoyed on a relatively short time frame.

This search for extra value takes organisations in a variety of directions - often depending on their current core customer base. The best are continually searching for the 'additional extra' that will appeal to that customer base.

IKEA, for example, has extended its recognition of 'family values' to its own stores.

IKEA loves families

Wide family parking spots

A baby care area

Microwaves

Shopping strollers

Play areas

(Let us know if there's anything else you need)

Lean

The Lean philosophy is an approach centred on the creation of value and the eradication of waste. Lean started in the Toyota Motor company in Japan but has since spread from its roots to be deployed in all industrial and commercial sectors.

Lean addresses a number of specific issues - but overall it looks at the value derived by each of the various processes in an organisation - and a process is a process, is a process … whether in a hospital, a hotel, a retail store, or a manufacturing plant.

It appeals to many people because of its simple and important focus on value and on the end customer - this also make its an attractive methodology for the hospitality sector where the 'customer is king'. We therefore support the adoption of the core principles of Lean to address productivity and performance improvement in the hospitality sector. Our 'executive summary' of the Lean philosophy is summed up below in the diagram and the text that immediately follows it.

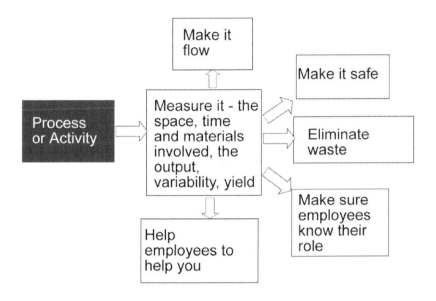

Measure it - it is important to know what is going on ... and to understand why. So we measure the process - and perhaps individual activities within it ... then we stand a much better chance of finding ways of reducing the space, time, materials involved.

Make it flow - we make sure the work is organised and laid out so that the materials flow logically along a defined path.

Make it safe and tidy - safe and tidy workplaces are also efficient workplaces!

Eliminate waste - we identify and then eliminate (or minimise) all sources of waste.

Make sure all employees understand their role - workers work better when they understand their role within the process, have the skills they need for that role, and understand the workplace rules.

Help employees help you improve - it is helpful to give employees the knowledge and tools they need to participate in improvement activity using Kaizen approaches.

The other 'principles' of Lean are that we do these things regularly and, when doing so, we make it all visible - simply.

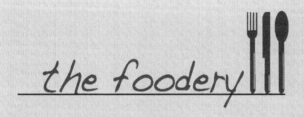

How would this apply to *the foodery*?

Well, one of the things that Darren and Paul should have done (and in fact, with the help of their consultant did do) was to design a range of processes for the key activities required to run a restaurant.

- What happens when a customer enters the restaurant?
- How do they get seated?
- How do diners waiting at the bar get informed when their table is ready?
- How do they get menus?
- Who takes their order?
- How is their order communicated to the kitchen?
- How does the kitchen announce that meals are ready?
- When should waiting staff check whether customers are ready for their next course?

… and so on.

Though these processes might be similar in all restaurants, they take place in a specific restaurant - with a particular layout, with particular technology, and with particular staff. The way in which people, information and food **flow** throughout the restaurant is really important. If the flow is wrong, errors or delays are likely to occur. So a useful exercise is to map the above processes onto the physical layout of the restaurant to show how they would work in practice ... and then think whether they will still work effectively and efficiently if the restaurant is full of drinkers and diners. How would flow change - for better or for worse - if we changed the table layout, the shape of tables, the size of tables, the size and shape of seating, the technology we use, etc.

Once we get *flow* right (at least temporarily as it needs to be checked from time to time as situations change), we turn our attention to *waste*.

Waste in Japanese is "muda" and to ensure that all waste is attacked, "muda" is broken down into 'the 7 wastes'. These are shown in Table 12-1.

These are conveniently re-ordered to make the acronym "TIM WOOD":

Transportation

Inventory

Motion

Waiting

Over-production

Over-processing

Defects

Over-production	Making too much or making things before they are needed
	'Just in case' instead of 'just in time' production
Waiting	Having goods waiting to be processed
	Do you enjoy queuing?
Transporting	Moving goods between processes
	This adds no value (and can cause damage or loss of quality)
Unnecessary Inventory	Storing parts and finished goods
	Work-in-progress can cover up scheduling problems but it is expensive and takes up space (which is also expensive)
Unnecessary or Excess Motion	Unnecessary bending, stretching, lifting, reaching
	Tiring, risky and takes up too much time
Defects	Throwing things away or repairing them because they aren't right
	So obviously wrong it needs no explanation!
Inappropriate processing	Using expensive tools, equipment and processing when simpler ones would do
	Using a sledgehammer to crack a nut!

Table 12-1: The 7 Wastes

In the hospitality sector , waste can occur at a number of points in the overall process and there are obvious and particular sources of waste relating to food preparation, cooking and disposal such as the loss of margin due to food knowingly being thrown away due to poor condition or being out of date and 'shrinkage'.

Shrinkage is the loss in margin due to unknown loss, possibly caused by poor stock management procedures, reporting practices and internal controls, including theft and infrequent and/or inaccurate stock control.

Both wastage and shrinkage are normally expressed as a percentage of sales and must be addressed. However, even a cursory look at the table of the 7 wastes shows that waste is about more than the wastage of materials - it is about doing things in ineffective or inefficient ways - adding costs to processes without increasing customer value. A simple example might be poor control of refrigeration - which can cost quite a bit of money in a large restaurant.

If waste is considered to be particularly important, then appropriate key performance indicators for waste should be included in the overall performance measurement programme.

Darren and Paul regularly walk round *the foodery* looking for :

- Areas with high inventory
- Areas which look a mess
- Piles of waste
- Piles of discarded packaging
- Damaged food
- Leaking taps/pipes
- Doors left open that could - and perhaps should - be closed
- Activities/ processes that consume large amounts of energy.

In fact, when the restaurant is closed, Darren sometimes walks round with a camera recording things that he can show to staff at the regular briefing sessions.

Remember ...

- In general terms, if something does not add value it must be waste ... and it must cost money! So, if we say THIS DOES NOT ADD VALUE, we try to identify what kind of waste it is.

Clean and Tidy = Safe and Productive

Untidy, cluttered work areas are not productive and not safe . They generate waste as people spend time searching for things (materials and implements) that are not in their 'correct' place. We want our workplaces to be both productive and safe.

Obviously, food-related premises must also be kept clean - and hygienic. In any case, customers, expect certain levels of cleanliness and tidiness - it is one of the criteria against which they will judge a restaurant (or hotel).

To ensure you maintain a safe and productive workplace you should:

- Have in place cleaning schedules and specified cleaning procedures for all work areas, all customer areas and all equipment

- Ensure that all food preparation and display areas are maintained using processes and procedures that conform to all rules and regulations
- Ensure that all staff are aware of all cleaning regimes and are trained to adhere to them
- Ensure that cleaning tools and equipment are maintained and that stocks of cleaning products and supplies are maintained
- Make sure that cleaning products are disposed of safely
- Ensure that all workplaces and workspaces are kept free of litter
- Ensure that no transport/movement routes are blocked by litter or discarded packaging
- Ensure that all staff are trained in maintaining personal cleanliness and hygiene
- Ensure that all staff are trained in basic health and safety awareness, are able to identify health and safety risks, are trained to report anything which might be considered a risk or might be considered offensive to customers (eg. Bad odours)
- Ensure there are procedures for the regular cleaning and servicing of toilet areas and washrooms.

Again as part of their regular 'waste walks', Darren and Paul look for:

- things which are out-of-place or untidy
- evidence that things which should be present actually are present (menus, self-service napkins and cutlery for example)
- evidence that all signage is up-to-date and clear to customers
- emergency exits that are obstructed in any way.

Whilst most restaurants can have checklists and procedures for undertaking this kind of check each day before the restaurant opens to customers, many modern restaurants are open almost 24 hours per day and this kind of inspection must be done on a regular basis throughout the day (and evening).

So, improving productivity and performance is largely a matter of 'common sense', looking for things that are happening that should not be happening, and looing for things that are not happening that should be happening. Methodologies, such as Lean, simply apply a discipline to this search for improvement but they are not a 'silver bullet'… they rely on the organization having clear, effective processes and procedures and using measurement (KPIs) to identify where things might be going wrong.

At *the foodery*, there have been some levels of dissatisfaction expressed at the menu. Alwoodley in Leeds is a curious, though not uncommon, mix of upwardly mobile, bright, young things and older, more conservative customers. Analysis of customer feedback forms shows that the older customers think the menu is too 'trendy' and are wanting something more 'traditional'. Kenneth is, of course, a little disappointed in this reaction but has been in the trade long enough to know that in terms of menu choice, 'the customer is always right'. A restaurant obviously has the right to make its own choices and to select that part of the market it wishes to attract, but Darren and Paul are keen to maintain a good spread of customers from all of those demographic groups that eat out regularly. They think this gives them more chance of surviving any downturn in the economy that affects specific social groups. They asked Kenneth to come up with a revised menu that could appeal across the board.

Kenneth, after some thought, decided that the two groups had fundamentally different requirements and so came up with a menu split into 2 sections which he has labeled 'Retro' (traditional food) and 'Metro' (more modern, more 'sophisticated' menu items). Darren and Paul have had these incorporated into a new printed menu that clearly shows this difference but attempts to do so without making it obvious who the intended client base is for each of the 2 sections. The new menu is currently being 'rolled out' and Darren and Paul have set up a special customer survey to judge initial customer reaction before deciding whether to 'fix' this as the new menu. This means, of course, that customer satisfaction becomes, at least temporarily, a clear Critical Performance Indicator since it is being used to establish whether fairly prompt control action is required before too much 'damage' is done.

This illustrates an important point. We use performance measures and indicators to help tell us where change might be necessary, and where improvement is taking place … and we use productivity/performance improvement tools and techniques (such as Lean) to help us improve - but ultimately it is the quality of the ideas that are generated which make real improvement happen. The measures and the tools offer a framework and set the context - but is the vision and the ideas that come from it that drive performance improvement.

John Heap, Tracy Todd & Mike Dillon

13 TECHNOLOGY IN THE HOSPITALITY SECTOR

As we have seen, hospitality aims to be efficient ... and responsive to customer need ...and much of that depends on collecting information and using it to react and respond. Additionally, of course, technology is used to underpin the efficient delivery of business processes. The range of technologies available to support the retail sector is wide ... and sometimes baffling.

One of the great developments over the last decade has been the growth of additional sales channels via the Internet so that a significant number of reservations and bookings (almost certainly, for most facilities, the majority) now takes place via computers and mobile phones.

One advantage of the move to Internet-based reservation is that it provides the service provider with useful information. The web analytics provide information on who is searching, from where, at what time. It is relatively easy to establish KPIs relating to such things as number of browsers who convert to customers, number of bookings abandoned before completion, etc. This can help improve the design of the online system.

In the future hotel and restaurant chains are going to have to understand all of the various ways in which a consumer engages with their company and their brand - basically the points at which a consumer 'touches' the brand. These various 'touch points' will form the basis of new hospitality 'ecosystems'. The options at these touch points also increase - for example, we have seen a mushrooming of payment options and partnerships.

Of course the fact that your customers have technology that allows them to reserve and buy from you online can create problems for you in other ways. We know that the young especially engage in a number of forms of social interaction on the web - blogging, tweeting and posting on Facebook for example. There is an old adage that if you provide good customer service to a customer, the customer will tell 2 people. If you provide poor customer service, that customer will tell 10 people. Using social media your disappointed customer can tell lots of people easily and simply and once the message is 'up', it is almost impossible to get it taken down. This is why customer service becomes ever more important.

We are used to paying by card, of course ... debit, credit and pre-paid cards but now in some restaurants and cafes stores, you can buy low-priced meals using your mobile phone - one 'problem' is that there are a number of competing systems and retailers have to take a decision as to which of the 'payment partnerships' they sign up with.

We talked earlier about the dissatisfaction of most customers with queues at reception or checkout desks. Many hotels have express checkout services where a pre-authorised credit card is used to pay any outstanding bill when a guest leaves without undertaking a physical checkout. Also, with modern, handheld terminals and cashless payment systems it is entirely feasible for a hotelier interested in maximising customer convenience and satisfaction to employ mobile staff who can attend to people in a queue and complete their transactions away from the checkout/till point.

Preventing losses

We have seen that waste, spoilage and shrinkage are all sources of financial loss. Most hospitality providers have a specific 'loss prevention' budget to try and curb such losses. Some of this budget will be spent on security personnel but some will be spent on security technology. Those that carry expensive stock items take extra care to protect their goods and there is a wide range of sensors and item tags available. RFID (Radio Frequency Identification) tagging is increasingly used to aid both stock management and security.

Airlines are starting to use RFID tags on customers' baggage to help ensure it gets to the right destination at the right time.

Barcodes have been a cornerstone of retail technology for a number of years, linking to point-of-sale systems and allowing much tighter control of inventory levels. Some retailers - especially clothing - and some hotel chains are now experimenting with RFID at the item level to replace barcodes (since the cost of tags is dropping). The great advantage of using RFID at the item level is that it is then present throughout the entire supply chain and can be used both to improve the efficiency of supply and to give improved customer service data.

Of course, some customers have privacy concerns about the ability of service providers to collect data on their buying habits and use it to target them with advertising and promotional offers … and companies should have a clear policy about the degree to which they maintain information at the level of the individual.

Knowing your customer

All service providers want to understand who their customers are … and what their buying preferences are. This is especially true for restaurateurs with a high frequency of customer interaction.

Basic things that they want to know are:

- Number of customers entering the restaurant
- How long customers stay
- What customers eat and drink.

This information is needed to answer such questions as:

- How many waiting staff do I need to operate at different times of the day/week/year?
- How can menus be changed at different times of the year to maximise customer spend?
- Is external and internal signage adequate to help customers have a pleasant experience and decide what they want from the restaurant?

Some of this is relatively easy to find out - some more difficult.

Some hotel and restaurant chains have experimented with loyalty schemes that aim to collect data on individuals and their purchase habits - creating sets of profiles which can be used as the basis of targeted advertising and promotional activity.

Helping your customer

Looking to the future, one can envisage a time when the personal digital assistants we have on our smartphones (think Siri on the iPhone) can be populated with a restaurant menu or hotel map as we enter so that we can ask our own assistant what is the 'Soup of the Day' or where the toilets are located.

Integrating information

It is clear from the above that large chains will have a lot of technology and numerous information systems and services. Food and beverage managers, rooms divisions managers and, of course, general managers all rely on these information systems to provide the information they need for planning and control. If organisations are not careful, these managers base their decisions on their 'own' information systems. In the worst possible case managers might take decisions on information that conflicts with that presented to another manager. This is typical 'silo' management. What is needed is integration of information systems - technically and functionally - so that information is captured once from the most appropriate and reliable source and then used throughout the integrated set of systems.

We talked earlier about the importance of measurement and of establishing a family or group of key and critical performance indicators that help balance priorities and viewpoints. This set of indicators should also help ensure the integration of information systems and services.

Energy Costs

There are some downsides to this widespread use of technology - in addition to the cost of procurement and maintenance. Increasingly large chains are concerned about the rising energy costs at their datacentres. Energy costs are rising faster than the cost of the hardware itself. In addition to the energy required to power the servers, since large server farms generate large quantities of heat; it is cooling that absorbs a lot of cost. Some companies have moved their datacentres to cooler climates to reduce this cooling bill.

To give an idea of what is possible with effective forward planning, Yahoo's latest facility, is in upstate New York. The buildings are oriented according to the prevailing winds that come off the Great Lakes, with vents along the walls and a high central cupola that allows waste heat to escape. The entire building is an air handler and servers are also laid out within it in order to maximize their fans' impact. As a result, the current estimate is that it will only require external cooling for 212 hours in an average year, which will be provided via evaporative cooling. Yahoo estimates that the cost to cool it will only be about a single per cent of what they were paying in their early, unplanned data centres.

What is clear is that chains need a technology strategy to underpin the information strategy they need to support the planning and control activities associated with their core merchandising and customer service strategies.

Communicating

Technology is not - as we have seen - something that stands alone. It serves to underpin the overall strategy and aims of the organisation. If an organisation has aims and aspirations in the areas of social and environmental performance, then they should be looking to technology to help deliver on those aspirations. Almost all aims and aspirations are promoted and secured through the provision of appropriate information. So, we are helped in reducing our energy costs (and the impact of our energy usage on the environment) by knowing what our costs are and where they are incurred. In terms of social development, we can improve the success of any social development programme by sharing information about the programme and its progress with the carious stakeholders.

Technology can also be used to 'police' areas of concern. We have already mentioned the use of CCTV and RFID to help in reducing losses but there are other ways in which we can use relatively simple technologies to improve our performance. Adidas, for example, is using the ubiquitous mobile phone to allow staff working in its supply chain to anonymously report (via SMS) instances of breach of compliance or other concerns direct to head office. Hopefully such systems are rarely used but such complementary communication channels can provide a useful backstop to more conventional channels.

John Heap, Tracy Todd & Mike Dillon

.

14 IMPLEMENTATION

We have taken you through a process that we know works. However, it has to be made to work each time ... it doesn't just happen. So as well as designing our system of KPIs/CPIs, our control actions, our reporting processes, our targets and our action plans for improvement, we have to implement them.

As with all change processes ... and all projects ... designing the outputs is not what matters. We can only generate success when we have successfully made the change or completed the project. Implementation is often the most difficult phase of a project ... but always a key phase.

First of all, we have to remember that our new system of PIs is going to impact upon a whole set of people. It is a change to their working arrangements. Their jobs and roles may not change but they will be acutely aware that their performance is being measured ... perhaps for the first time in such a formal way.

Resistance to Change

New - and almost certainly revised or updated - performance measurement and management systems, of any kind, will be viewed with suspicion by those being measured ... or those who think they are being measured. (Remember it is usually the system or process that is being measured - but that system process involves people and they well feel that it is their individual or team performance that is subject to scrutiny.)   After all, we are trying to change their behaviour ... and one assumes they behave the way they do currently because they feel it appropriate in the light of their current reading of 'their situation'.

The three commonest reasons underlying resistance to change are:

- ▶ **A fear of the unknown**
- ▶ **Comfort with the present situation**
- ▶ **A lack of awareness of what the change is and why it is necessary.**

Those who have worked in a particular department or on a particular process for some time have developed techniques and skills to help them carry out that work. They are naturally fearful that any change destroys any advantage that their skill and experience gives them ... and thus lowers their value to the organisation. In our case we are not necessarily making any changes to the process - simply adding some measurement to it - but this itself can be threatening. "What is the measurement for? What happens if my performance is poor... if I fail?"

Evans (1996) suggests that this kind of fear is particularly true of non-profit organisations who may see initial employee resistance and even a resulting initial spike in labour turnover. However, Evans does suggest that performance management is a critical issue for such organisations as competition for donor funds increases and suggests that effective consultation with staff, so that they can see that the particular mission and values of the organisation is reflected in the nature of the performance management being proposed, can minimise any resistance .... and can even be shown to be beneficial to both the organisation and the employees.

The same is obviously true of for-profit (and all other) organisations including hotels. Remember we said earlier that one of the principles of an effective performance indicator is that "everyone should know it matters". Now is the time to deliver on that principle. So, we must make it clear that we are measuring 'things that matter' and we must take the time and make the effort to ensure that employees (and especially those who roles and jobs are being subject to measurement processes) understand why it matters. Depending on the CSF/PIs this could apply to staff constantly in front of the guests and those in the back office. All should have a clear stake in the success of the hotel/business.

Most people go through a set of responses in different phases when reacting to change. When they first hear about possible change they become fearful. As it gets nearer they may (individually or collectively) become confrontational. As the change happens they remember what they are losing and may become depressed (not clinically depressed but 'sad' about what they are giving up). They at some stage reach grudging acceptance … and hopefully finally reach a stage where they 'see the light'. They understand why the change was necessary and realise that they have not lost all they thought they would lose; in fact, often they realise they have gained.

The aim of those managing the change is to move people through these phases as quickly as possible. This is done mainly through effective communication throughout the whole process. We need to ensure - at each stage of the change - that everyone involved - from those operating the processes being measured, through those taking the measurements, to those receiving the reported data and acting upon it know what is happening …. and why. At the end of the process there is a need to check that this has been done effectively … that people are starting to 'see the light'.

It may also be possible to improve communication processes by using some of those subject to the change to help in the process - by convincing a small number of key influencers and letting them communicate to the rest of the workforce.

ABC Engineering installed a plantwide measurement system as part of an incentive payment scheme - which offered extra pay in return for improved group performance. The project was a joint venture between management and the trade union and they worked together for several months to select and fine-tune the measures to be used. Managers initially worried that 'opening the books' to the union might be dangerous, even though they contained operational rather than financial information.

Some (mainly older) managers thought the union wouldn't understand the information, so there was no real problem; some of the younger managers were worried that the union might only partially understand the information and that this might lead to difficulties at bargaining time.

In fact, a few of the union workers were able to combine a working knowledge of accounting (learnt from outside interests) with a deep knowledge of plant operations .... and easily matched the understanding of many of the managers.

The measurement system was launched successfully and proved so successful in operation that it became a model for organisations elsewhere. When the company gave presentations on the systems, a manager introduced the 'whys' and a union member talked about the 'hows'.

So, the best way to minimise any possible resistance to the changes you want to make is to treat the 'audience' with respect and communicate the nature of, and the reasons for, the changes to them clearly and often.

Performance measurement should not be something done to the workforce but something done in partnership with the workforce. It should be clear that what is being measured is the output of 'the system' or 'the process', not the output or quality levels of individuals or teams. After all, if the quantity or quality of work produced by a worker is unsatisfactory, it is as likely to be a failure of training or the result of an inappropriate work rate, as it is a specific failing of the worker.

It is possible that, despite your best efforts, there will still be 'pockets of resistance' amongst certain individuals or groups. One common approach in such cases is to ask people to accept the change on a pilot or trial basis ... and to undertake this trial over a reasonably long time period.

The theory is that either:

a) **They will see the system in action and realise that it is both non-threatening to them and helpful to the organisation;**

and/or

b) **The changed (pilot) situation becomes the 'status quo' to be protected; i.e. they resist the change back to the original situation.**

Usually, however, if you are open and transparent about the need for, and the nature of, the measurement process, resistance will be minimised.

Implementation Strategy

We have said before that this project is not something we can afford to get wrong. It would be useful if we could 'try it out' somewhere else. This is not normally possible. However, this has process has been implemented in other industries and educational establishments.

From it, it was found the GM and the board had to be strongly supportive and act as powerful advocates for the implementation process. However, the indicators being implemented must be genuinely 'key' and 'critical' (though perhaps not a complete set) or the leadership team will not be focused and committed.

If we design, prepare and implement well ... we should have a success. Time to relax? Well, of course we are too busy managing the operation of the project to relax. And we do have one step of the whole process left.

Step 9: Review

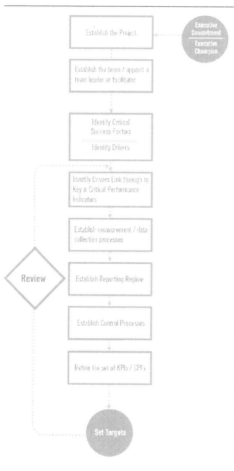

No system of PIs will last for ever - it should be reviewed regularly to make sure that the CSFs have not changed (with changing hotel - or political - priorities).

Also, a well-designed set of PIs often has to strike a balance among several measures whilst maintaining a creative tension among them.

This is because there are choices or tradeoffs forced between different elements - quality and cost, timeliness and documentation, etc. Over time this tension can be dissipated because the organisation has learnt to live with a particular set of measures and knows which to ignore (because the real priority is ...).

This suggests that one or more of the 'PIs' is not really 'key' and the set of PIs should be reviewed and adjusted.

Review is needed at relatively short intervals - perhaps every 6 months. After all, one of the questions we suggested you should ask when determining your critical success factors was:

What do we want to have happen in this time period if we can concentrate on only a few things?

This suggests - quite rightly - that CSFs and PIs might change regularly as the strategic priorities of the hotel/business change, or as the environment in which it operates changes. It is, anyway, an advantage to have changes in the measurement regime as it helps prevent complacency arising from the (over-) familiarity with the set of indicators that gets published regularly.

Similarly, the set of PIs should be subjected to the CEO/GM test at regular intervals. Is the GM actually taking notice of the PIs. Does he/she want the figures on his/her desk every morning/week? If not, is he/she asking for other data which is regarded as 'more important'? If so, the PIs that are being ignored or downgraded might have outlived their usefulness. Perhaps they were once key or critical … but now they no longer are.

Of course another critical question is ..

Has the use of the KPIs - and the actions that lead from them - led to measurable improvement in our performance?

We are not measuring, setting targets and designing change programmes to occupy ourselves - but to make a difference to the productivity and performance of the organization. If that change is not forthcoming the 'system' isn't working and we need to go back to the drawing board.

Cautionary note

We have worked through this process as if it was a simple, linear process … but things are rarely that simple. This is a 'model' that will need reviewing and refining for each specific implementation. It will certainly vary with the skills and experience of the facilitator and any external adviser … and may need adjustment in different types of hotel or restaurant. However the overall model contains all the key steps that should enable you to create a set of key and critical performance indicators that should allow you both to control your establishment/organization on an ongoing basis - and identify opportunities for growth and further success.

Reference

Evans, A., 1996. Performance management. *Seminars for Nurse Managers*, 10(2), p.639.

EPILOGUE

If you are still reading this book in a bookshop - go, get a life … or preferably, go buy the book. Although it is (deliberately) short, it needs a bit of thinking to accompany the reading.

You should read the first few chapters so you know what needs to be done.

When you are ready to go ahead with a project to create a set of Key and Critical Performance Indicators (because you know how important they can be), work through the *Getting It Done* section.

Key Lessons

Critical Success Factors are those things you have to do - and do well - to survive, prosper and grow.

Key and Critical Performance Indicators are the measures that tell you how well you are doing in relation to those Critical Success Factors.

All Critical Performance Indicators are Key Performance Indicators but not all Key Performance Indicators are Critical Performance Indicators.

Key and Critical Performance Indicators 'touch' the whole hotel/restaurant – so, during your project, the whole place should be made aware of what is going on - and why.

The project needs the support of the CEO/GM and Board, (if there is one), to make sure nothing stops it from happening.

The project needs to be team-based so that different departments and sections of the hotel/restaurant come together to create a holistic view of performance.

The team needs an effective facilitator/leader.

The team might need some external expertise and advice.

The team needs to work through a structured process and (luckily) we have supplied one.

We live in a dynamic world where the environment changes regularly (thank you, government). The PIs you create today may not be the ones you need tomorrow. Keep them under review.

Good luck!

INDEX

ABOUT THE AUTHORS

Professor **Mike Dillon** is Chief Executive of the Institute of Productivity and is a world-renowned expert on manufacturing strategy and on the seafood sector. Recently Mike has been involved in a number of major international projects, working with the United Nations Industrial Development Organisation.

Mike is Vice-President of the World Network of Productivity Organizations; a Fellow of the World Academy of Productivity Science; Senior Research Fellow at Grimsby Institute in the UK; and Secretary of IAFI, the association of seafood professionals.

John Heap is Managing Director of the Institute of Productivity; President of the World Confederation of Productivity Science; President of the European Association of National Productivity Centres; visiting professor at Srinivas Institute of Management Studies in Mangalore, India; co-editor of the International Journal of Productivity & Performance Management; a Member of Council of the Institute of Management Services; a Member of the Advisory Board of the Institute for Consultancy and Productivity Research (India); and a director of Juice e-Learning.

John, like Mike, is the author of a number of books and journal articles and a regular keynote presenter at international conferences.

Tracy Todd is a Researcher and Development Consultant at the Institute of Productivity. Tracy has a strong history of international consultancy and innovative leadership, with a background in the retail and hospitality sectors. Furthermore, she has extensive experience in the Middle East & North Africa giving her a particular understanding of strategic and operational change within different economic, social and cultural contexts.

John Heap, Tracy Todd & Mike Dillon

Made in the USA
Charleston, SC
19 November 2014